OECD Public Governance Reviews

Integrity Framework for Public Investment

Please cite this publication as:
OECD (2016), *Integrity Framework for Public Investment*, OECD Public Governance Reviews, OECD Publishing, Paris.
http://dx.doi.org/10.1787/9789264251762-en

ISBN 978-92-64-25175-5 (print)
ISBN 978-92-64-25176-2 (PDF)

Series: OECD Public Governance Reviews
ISSN 2219-0406 (print)
ISSN 2219-0414 (online)

Photo credits: Cover © nattanan726/Shutterstock.com.

Corrigenda to OECD publications may be found on line at: *www.oecd.org/about/publishing/corrigenda.htm*.

Foreword

Investment - whether funded publicly, privately, or jointly - can be a driver of sustainable economic growth and development, and is necessary for the provision of basic services. However, given the often impressive monetary and political gains at stake, investment, and particularly infrastructure investment, can also be vulnerable to capture and corruption. Indeed, large-scale infrastructure projects are, unfortunately, often associated with political pandering, bribery, and collusion. Recent evidence from the OECD Foreign Bribery Report, for instance, found that almost 60% of foreign bribery cases occurred in four sectors related to infrastructure.

Where incentives for misconduct are high, the resulting damage is considerable, and governments and citizens alike ultimately pay the price for the acts of a few officials or firms. Moreover, governments suffer not only financially but also in terms of trust and confidence lost: failed public investments are highly visible blunders. These "white elephants", as they are called, are difficult for citizens to forget, or forgive. Unused stadiums, roads and buildings are daily reminders of their misspent taxes.

To help governments avoid such cases and maintain citizens' trust, the OECD has developed an **Integrity Framework for Public Investment**. High standards of conduct, policies for identifying and managing conflict of interest, strong internal and external controls and greater transparency are the main weapons in governments' arsenals to combat corruption. At the same time, they ensure that the competitive processes that keep costs low and quality high work effectively.

The Framework was initially discussed during the **2015 OECD Integrity Forum**, and has benefited from an open consultation with stakeholders. It includes concrete measures and mechanisms that can be employed at each phase of the public investment cycle in order to safeguard integrity. Examples of good implementation practices from both the public and private sectors are provided for consideration and inspiration.

The Framework arrives at a most opportune moment, as countries face widening infrastructure gaps following the economic crisis. Public infrastructure is a prime candidate for investment as a driver of productivity and growth. Furthermore, public investment can help reduce inequalities by offering better access to public services and levelling the playing field for firms. Corruption-free and productive public investments will be central to a speedy and more inclusive recovery.

Rolf Alter

OECD Director for Public Governance and Territorial Development

Acknowledgements

The *Integrity Framework for Public Investment* was prepared by the Public Sector Integrity Division of the OECD Directorate for Public Governance and Territorial Development.

Under the guidance of Janos Bertók and Julio Bacio Terracino, this report was drafted by Emma Cantera, Minjoo Son, Natalia Nolan Flecha with input from Sofia Wickberg and Jeroen Michels.

Special thanks go to those experts who provided input and comments on the Framework, namely Neill Stansbury, Co-founder and Director of the Global Infrastructure Anti-Corruption Centre, Christiaan Poortman, Chair of the Construction Sector Transparency Initiative and Jill Wells from Engineers Against Poverty.

We benefited from comments from the Divisions on Regulatory Policy and Regional Development Policy and valuable inputs were also received from the OECD Directorate for Financial and Enterprise Affairs (Investment Division, Anti-Corruption Division, Corporate Affairs Division), the OECD Development Co-operation Directorate (Global Partnerships and Policies Division) and the Business and Industry Advisory Committee to the OECD.

Particular appreciation also goes to those who participated in the debate on the framework during the OECD Integrity Forum, *Curbing Corruption - Investing in Growth,* held on 25-26 March 2015, namely H.E. Mr. Lee Sungbo, Chair, Anti-Corruption and Civil Rights Commission of Korea; Gabriela Ramos, Chief of Staff, OECD; Axel Threlfall, Editor-at-Large, Reuters; Giovanni Kessler, Director-General, European Anti-Fraud Office (OLAF); Cobus de Swardt, Managing Director, Transparency International; Nadia van der Merwe, Associate Director, Control Risks; Adrian Blundell-Wignall, Director, Directorate for Financial and Enterprise Affairs, OECD; Pavlos Eleftheriadis, Associate Professor of Law, Oxford University; Klaus Moosmayer, Chief Compliance Officer, Siemens and Chair of the BIAC Anti-Bribery Task Force; Sheila Krumholz, Executive Director, Center for Responsive Politics; Bob Rijkers, Economist, World Bank; A. Craig Copetas, Correspondent-at-Large, Quartz/Atlantic Media; Juan Yermo, Deputy Chief of Staff, OECD; Tina Søreide, Postdoc Researcher in Law and Economics, University of Bergen; M. Emranul Haque, Senior Lecturer, University of Manchester; Phil Mason, Chair of the Anti-Corruption Task Team, OECD; Elizabeth Hart, International Consultant; Joshua Drew, Vice President of Ethics, HP; Erik Feiring, Policy Officer, World Bank; Phil Tarling, Executive Committee Member and former Chair of the Board, Institute of Internal Auditors; Pierre Poret, Deputy Director, Directorate for Financial and Enterprise Affairs, OECD; Anders Berg, Deputy Director-General, Norwegian Ministry of Trade and Industry and Chair, OECD Working Party on State Ownership and Privatisation Practices; Sagarika Chatterjee, Associate Director, UN Principles for Responsible Investment; Corinne Lagache, Senior Vice President, Group Compliance Officer, Safran and Vice-Chair, BIAC Anti-Bribery Task Force; Aneta McCoy, Founder and Managing

Partner, Aneta McCoy Advisory Group; Ade Onitolo, Deputy Head of Commercial and Economic Diplomacy Department, Foreign and Commonwealth Office, United Kingdom; Peder Michael Pruzan-Jorgensen, Vice President for Europe, Middle East and Asia, Business Social Responsibility (BSR); Vladimir Khvalei, Vice President of the ICC International Court of Arbitration; Catherine Kessedjian, Arbitrator, Professor, Université Panthéon-Assas; Lauri Railas, Attorney, Railas Attorneys Ltd.; Joachim Pohl, Policy Analyst, Investment Division, OECD; H.E. Mr. Raffaele Cantone, President of the Italian National Anti-Corruption Authority; Roel Nieuwenkamp, Chair of the OECD Working Party on Responsible Business Conduct; Christiaan Poortman, Chair, CoST Interim Board; Enrico Vink, Managing Director, International Federation of Consulting Engineers; Augusto Goncalves Ferradaes, Federal Auditor, Brazilian Federal Court of Accounts; Viviane Schiavi, Senior Policy Manager, International Chamber of Commerce; Carlos Santiso, Division Chief, Institutional Capacity of the State Division, Inter-American Development Bank (IDB); Fuad Khoury Zarzar, Comptroller General, Peru; Victor Hard, Trinidad and Tobago EITI Steering Committee; Juan Cruz Vieyra, Operations Specialist, IDB; Lahra Liberti, Senior Advisory on Natural Resources, OECD Development Centre; Robert Leventhal, Director of Anti-Crime Programs, US Department of State; Anwar Shah, Advisor to the World Bank and the Asian Development Bank, Director of the Centre for Public Economics, and Distinguished Visiting Professor of Economics, Southwestern University of Finance and Economics, Chengdu/Wenjiang; Kristien Verbraeken, Integrity Officer, Public Governance Department, Corporate HR and Organisational Development Division, Belgium; Pierre Berthet, Former Auditor at the Regional Chamber of Accounts Provence-Alps-Côte d'Azur, Senior Advisor, Central Service for Preventing Corruption, French Ministry of Justice; Bert Kuby, Head of Unit, EU Committee of the Regions; Patrick Moulette, Head, Anti-Corruption Division, OECD; Richard Bistrong, Anti-Bribery, Compliance and Ethics Consultant; Philippe Montigny, CEO and President of the Certification Committee, Ethic Intelligence; Enery Quinones, Former Chief Compliance Officer, European Bank for Reconstruction and Development; Richard Alderman, Former Director, UK Serious Fraud Office; Rolf Alter, Director, Directorate for Public Governance and Territorial Development, OECD; H.E. Mr. Dionisio Pérez-Jácome Friscione, Ambassador, Mexican Delegation to the OECD; H.E. Ms. Annika Markovic, Amassador, Swedish Delegation to the OECD; H.E. Mr. Nick Bridge, UK Delegation to the OECD; Drago Kos, Chair of the OECD Working Group on Bribery; Robert Hunja, Director for Public Integrity and Openness, Governance Global Practice, World Bank; Elena Panfilova, Vice-Chair, Transparency International; H.E. Mr. Aivaras Abromaicius, Minister of Economic Development and Trade, Ukraine.

Table of contents

Figures

Executive summary

"Corruption is one of the most toxic impediments to efficient and effective investment."

- Angel Gurría, OECD Secretary-General, 2015 OECD Integrity Forum

Public infrastructure is a common good, with positive direct and indirect benefits for the economy and society as a whole

Investment is public or private expenditure that adds to the public and private physical capital stock. This includes fixed assets such as dwellings (excluding land), other buildings and structures (roads, bridges, airports and dams), transport equipment, machinery, cultivated assets, and intangible fixed assets (such as intellectual property). Investment is a driver for sustainable growth and development. It is essential for the provision of basic services such as electricity, water and sanitation and is also a requisite for the delivery of public services like health, education and security.

Investment constitutes a significant share of the gross domestic product (GDP) in OECD countries, close to 20% on average. Although, mainly private (about 15% is public), governments have a central role to play in infrastructure investment. Infrastructure is a public good insofar as it is predominantly non-excludable and non-rival in consumption, and as such is best provided for by public authorities. In addition, public investment can be thought of as a type of policy tool by which governments can promote sustainable economic growth, innovation, and contribute to well-being through the provision of basic infrastructure and public services. Indeed, governments use public investment, and especially investment in infrastructure, to respond to a variety of policy challenges. It has the potential to boost economic performance, increase productivity and generate aggregate demand, by improving human capital and encouraging technological innovation.

Many countries are facing infrastructure gaps, both in terms of quantity and quality

Expenditures to build new infrastructure or maintain old ones have generally not kept pace with countries' needs, with this challenge having been identified as one of the main factors that slow down economic recovery and hinder development efforts. Indicators suggest that a wide gap exists between infrastructure availability and the need for it, particularly in emerging economies and low-income developing countries. The infrastructure gap is not exclusively a question of quantity; the quality of infrastructure should also be taken into account. The requirement for infrastructure investment is a concern for advanced economies as well; signs of deteriorating quality of infrastructure have been recorded in recent years. A large percentage of public investment goes to maintenance costs associated with past infrastructure investments.

Avoiding capture in public investment is essential to maximise its benefits

Against this background, simply increasing the amount of public spending in infrastructure is not necessarily the solution; Public investment must be productive and efficient in order to achieve real economic and social value, and to contribute to building sustainable and inclusive growth. Influence by vested interests in the decision may result even in negative return of productivity or excessive infrastructure, creating "white elephant" projects.

The nature of public investment in infrastructure makes it particularly prone to corruption

Bribery, policy capture, embezzlement, abuse of functions, and trading in influence are common examples of corrupt acts, although the exact legal definitions of these vary across countries. Corruption allegations concerning government-financed infrastructure projects are common. Indeed, the extent of public officials' discretion over the investment decision, the large sums of money involved, and the multiple stages and stakeholders implicated contribute to making them more vulnerable to undue influence.

Corruption creates extra burdens and costs on investment, which reduces value for money and the quality of results

Corruption comes with a high cost. Direct costs include bribe transfers, higher expenses, scarcity of essential services, lower quality and misallocation of public funds. Corruption also incurs more subtle indirect costs, such as lower incentives to innovate if market opportunities or jobs are allocated on other grounds than qualifications, the effect of not receiving the government services one is entitled to, lower trust in government institutions and adverse selection of contractors. The costs of fraud and corruption in public investment are not only economic, but also institutional and political, with serious implications for the legitimacy of the state apparatus and the ability of elected leaders and government institutions to function effectively.

Towards a comprehensive, coherent and focused policy framework to promote integrity in public investment for sustainable economic growth

The *Integrity Framework for Public Investment* aims to assist governments and private sector actors in mitigating corruption risks in public investment by identifying corruption entry points over the entire public investment cycle. The framework identifies tools and mechanisms to promote integrity in public investment, including measures for promoting ethical standards, managing conflict of interest, strengthening monitoring and controls, and increasing transparency.

The instrument can be applied at national and sub-national levels and across sectors, including transport, construction, extractive industries, and energy supply, taking into account the needs and characteristics of the specific investment at stake.

Chapter 1

Integrity in public investment for sustainable economic growth

Public investment is an essential element for sustainable economic growth which also could result in significant consequences when it is not properly carried out. In this regard, avoiding capture in public investment projects is crucial in order to maximise its economic and social benefits. Building on this idea, this chapter maps out the integrity risks associated with each phase of the public investment cycle in order to appropriately address the integrity risks resulting from the complexity and the multiple stakeholders involved in public investment projects.

The statistical data for Israel are supplied by and under the responsibility of the relevant Israeli authorities. The use of such data by the OECD is without prejudice to the status of the Golan Heights, East Jerusalem and Israeli settlements in the West Bank under the terms of international law.

Public investment constitutes a sizeable share of total investment spending

Defining public investment is not as clear cut as it seems. It is commonly defined as public expenditure that adds to the public physical capital stock. This would include such fixed assets as dwellings (excluding land), other buildings and structures (roads, airports, bridges, dams, telecommunications structures, utilities, government office buildings, schools, hospitals, prisons, etc.), transport equipment, machinery, cultivated assets, and intangible fixed assets such as intellectual property. Ordinary maintenance of fixed assets is not generally accounted for as investment, unless it constitutes a major improvement with a demonstrably high impact on performance or capacity. As the majority of public investment refers to physical infrastructure investment, this framework refers interchangeably to public infrastructure and public investment carried out by national and sub-national levels.

Public investment can be thought of as a type of policy tool by which governments can promote sustainable economic growth, innovation, and contribute to well-being through the provision of basic infrastructure and public services. Indeed, governments use public investment, and particularly investment in infrastructure, to respond to a variety of policy challenges before them, from climate change, to economic downturns, changing demographic trends, rapid urbanisations and the emergence of new technologies. As noted by the European Investment Bank, "well-functioning infrastructure networks are the backbone of prospering economies" (European Investment Bank, 2010). Public investment is indeed fundamental to economic and social well-being since it contributes to the national capital stock by allocating resources to basic infrastructure (such as transport, energy and water distribution or communication channels), innovative activity (research and technology), ecologically-friendly investments (clean power sources), and education that leads to higher productivity and living standards (Economic Policy Institute, 2012). With such important policy goals at stake, investments carried out with integrity maximise their impact and ensure the productive and efficient use of public resources.

In 2013, across OECD member countries, general government investment as a share of total investment in the economy (both public and private investment combined) reached an average of 15.6% (OECD, 2015a) (Figure 1.1). This amounted to about USD 1.4 trillion (OECD, 2015b). In terms of total general government spending, this investment constituted just over 7% of expenditures in the same year (Figure 1.1). Sub-national governments play a key role in public investment, as they undertook approximately 60% of these outlays (OECD, 2015a) (Figure 1.2).

Figure 1.1. **General government investment as a share of total investment and total general government expenditure, 2013**

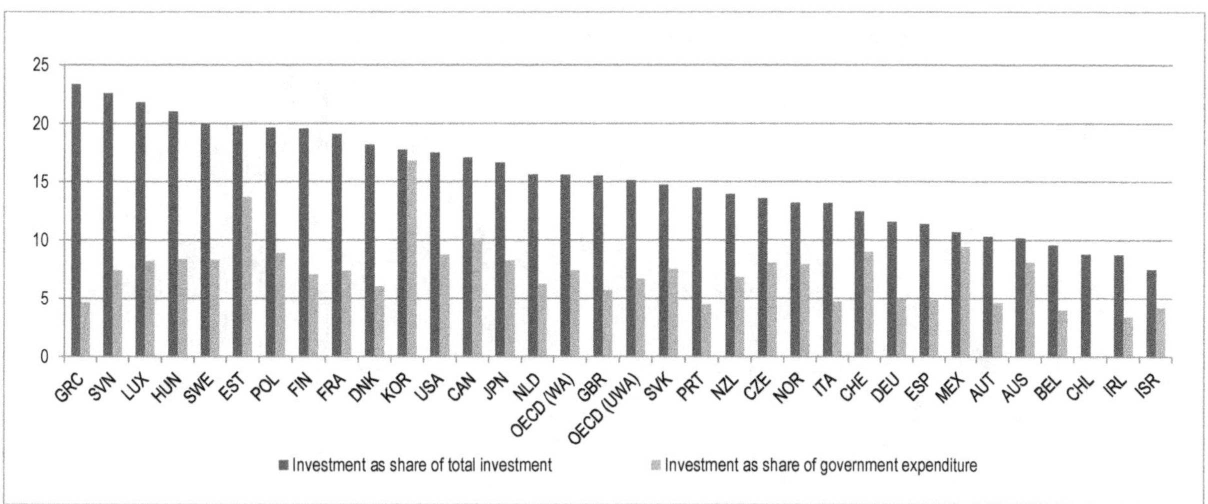

Note: Data refer to general government spending, excluding public corporations which, in many countries, are often involved in public infrastructure projects. Therefore these data may underestimate the total amount of public investment. OECD (WA) refers to the OECD weighted average, and OECD (UWA) to the unweighted average.

The statistical data for Israel are supplied by and under the responsibility of the relevant Israeli authorities. The use of such data by the OECD is without prejudice to the status of the Golan Heights, East Jerusalem and Israeli settlements in the West Bank under the terms of international law.

Source: OECD (2015b), *OECD National Accounts Statistics* (database), http://dx.doi.org/10.1787/na-data-en (accessed on 20 October 2015).

Public infrastructure is a common good with positive direct and indirect benefits for the economy and society as a whole

Governments have a central role to play in infrastructure investment. Infrastructure is a public good considering that it is predominantly non-excludable and non-rival in consumption, and that it is best provided for by public authorities. Although infrastructure is historically featured within the public realm, since the mid-20th century, it entered into a new phase of increased partnership with the private sector through privatisations, new regulations and new co-operation channels supported by innovative legal frameworks leading to some infrastructure projects being fully financed and operated by the private sector (European Investment Bank, 2010). The tight fiscal space faced by many governments, especially following the recent crisis, does not always allow them to fund all productive and necessary infrastructure investments. In addition, the infrastructure gaps that are, and will be faced in the coming decades, increasingly underscore the need for private investment. However, governments remain the main player in infrastructure provision as it is still for governments to decide on what to invest. It is, therefore, crucial that public investment is planned so as to benefit society as a whole and with a long-term vision, and that its management is not co-opted for the benefit of private interests.

Figure 1.2. **Distribution of investment spending across levels of government, 2013**

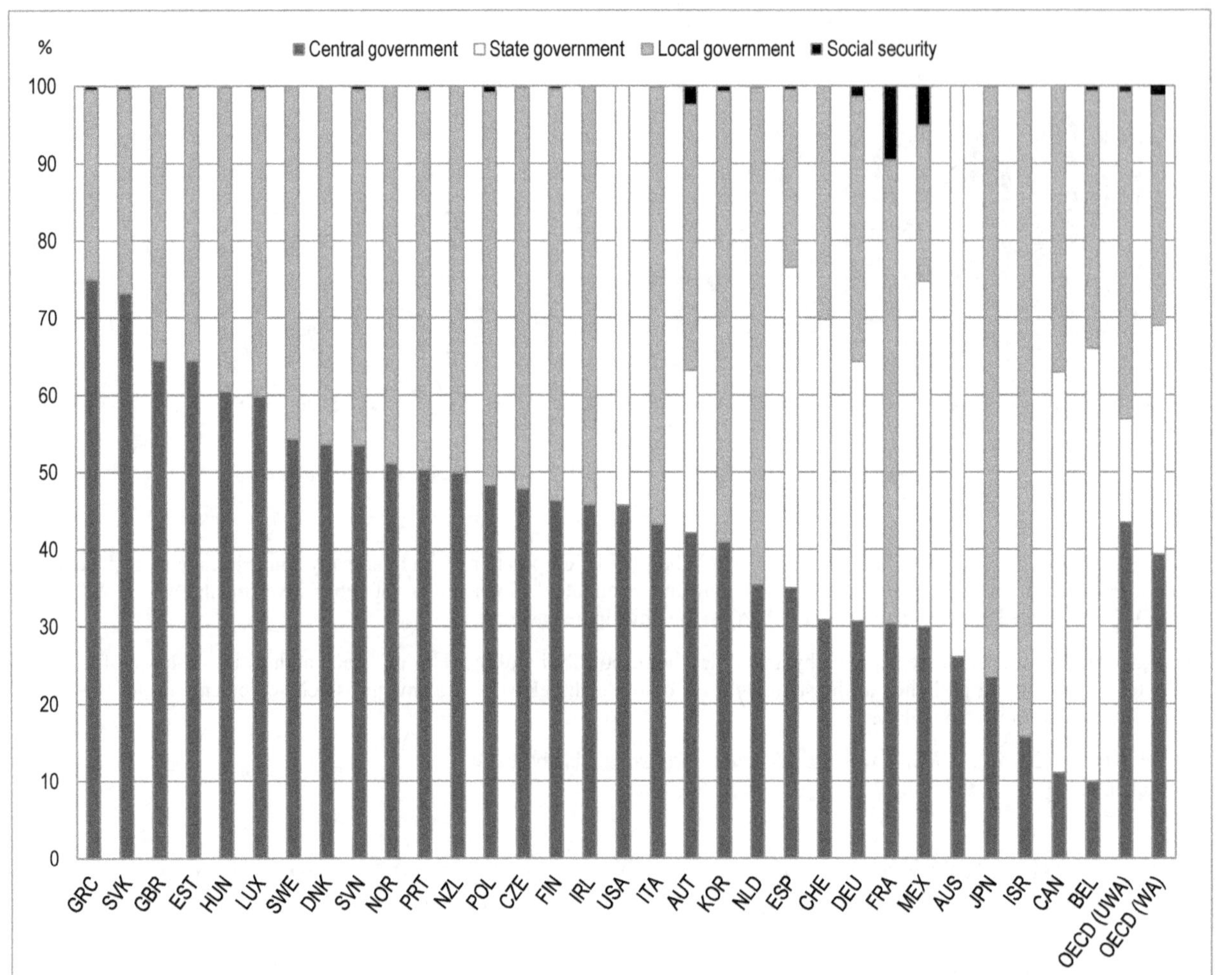

Note: Data refers to general government spending, excluding public corporations which, in many countries, are often involved in public infrastructure projects. Therefore these data may underestimate the total amount of public investment. OECD (WA) refers to the OECD weighted average, and OECD (UWA) to the unweighted average.

The statistical data for Israel are supplied by and under the responsibility of the relevant Israeli authorities. The use of such data by the OECD is without prejudice to the status of the Golan Heights, East Jerusalem and Israeli settlements in the West Bank under the terms of international law.

Source: OECD (2015b), *OECD National Accounts Statistics* (database), http://dx.doi.org/10.1787/na-data-en (accessed on 20 October 2015).

While smaller in comparison to other types of government outlays, such as social welfare spending (e.g. unemployment and other social benefits), public investment nevertheless "packs a punch", potentially creating both direct benefits as well as positive externality gains for the economy and society as a whole. Public (or publicly funded) infrastructure like transport and telecommunication networks provide a direct benefit by ensuring that the necessary infrastructure is in place for commerce and trade, and allowing economic activity to reach remote areas. Likewise, public investment has direct benefits such as the delivery of basic services (e.g. water and sanitation) as well as the delivery of social services (e.g. education, health, and security).

Positive externalities of these investments include increased productivity; the promotion of innovation and employment creation; as well as potential benefits for the environment, all of which contribute both to sustainable economic growth and greater well-being (Straub, 2008). Indeed, schools and hospitals are not only bricks and mortar - they are the necessary infrastructure required for bettering human capital and improving quality of life (Economic Policy Institute, 2012). Likewise, law enforcement uses public infrastructure to deliver services such as safety and security, which are precursors to many other outcomes including social stability and creating an enabling environment for doing business. Moreover, investments in renewable energy infrastructure, such as photovoltaic installations and offshore wind farms, often combine positive employment, economic and environmental externalities. The World Bank Enterprise Survey shows that poor public infrastructure is considered a hindrance to doing business by private companies.

The need for infrastructure not only refers to quantity shortage, but more precisely better quality

Insufficient infrastructure investment has been cited as one of the major challenges impeding development and a speedy recovery following the economic crisis. Estimates show that "USD 57 trillion in infrastructure investment will be required between 2013 and 2030 – simply to keep up with projected global GDP growth" (McKinsey Global Institute, 2013). Standard and Poor's has valued annual funding needs for infrastructure at USD 3.4 trillion annually with most of that evenly split among the United States, the European Union, and China (Standard and Poor's, 2014). Similarly, it is estimated that Asia will need to spend approximately USD 8 trillion in order to maintain current levels of economic growth (PWC, 2012).

Other indicators suggest that a wide gap exists between infrastructure availability and need (Table 1.1). This is a serious concern, particularly for emerging market economies and low-income developing countries. Lack of access to water and basic sanitation, as well as electricity shortages, still exist, all of which require infrastructure investment. Infrastructure is also needed to keep up with predicted world population growth, which is estimated to increase by 27% by 2075, reaching 9.22 billion inhabitants (UN, 2009). Most of that increase will come from less developed regions, thereby enhancing the need for new economic infrastructure in the areas of energy, water, sanitation, transportation, as well as in social infrastructure such as schools and hospitals. Taken together, annual investment requirements for telecommunications, road, rail, electricity (transmission and distribution) and water have been estimated to account for 2.5% of world gross domestic product (GDP) (OECD, 2007a).

Table 1.1. **Estimated requirements for infrastructure spending in coming years**

Region	Estimated requirement for infrastructure spending
Worldwide	USD 20.7 trillion would be required today if all governments simultaneously decided to enact over 1 400 policies to secure energy supplies due to decades of underinvestment in energy infrastructure
East Asia	USD 700 billion per year for the next ten years
South Asia	USD 88 billion per year for the next ten years
Western Europe	USD 600 billion between now and 2020 for transport
Africa	USD 40 billion annually for investment and operations and maintenance
OECD countries and some larger developing countries (such as Brazil, China and India)	USD 70 trillion between 2005–07 and 2030 for surface transportation (roads, rail and urban public transport), water, telecommunications, electricity transmission, distribution and generation and other energy-related infrastructure
Developing and transitional countries	USD 80 billion annually will be required in the next 25 years to produce water security
Emerging economies	USD 22 trillion in projected investments over the next ten years

Source: Adapted from UNCTAD (2009), "The role of public investment in social and economic development", http://unctad.org/en/Docs/webdiae20091_en.pdf.

The requirement for infrastructure is also a concern for advanced economies, although the focus of the infrastructure gap in this sense is on the quality of the infrastructure (Figure 1.3). Within these advanced economies, signs of deteriorating quality of infrastructure have been identified in recent years (Figure 1.4). Indeed, EU countries for example have spent 70% of their public investment on maintenance costs associated with past infrastructure investments (OECD, 2014a). The need for infrastructure in OECD countries is significant, where key infrastructure such as bridges and tunnels are more than a century old. Furthermore, there is a widespread concern that spending on maintenance has been lower than ideal, further raising concerns about an increase in expected future infrastructure maintenance costs. In Germany, for example, the report of the Daehre Commission notes that road infrastructure investments in the country have declined from 1% of GDP to around 0.7% in recent years (Daehre, 2012). Gross expenditures have declined by 24% in real terms over the past 20 years. Over that same period, passenger traffic increased by a quarter and freight traffic by a factor of three. Quality indicators show a marked decline. Under current funding arrangements, available resources fall short by EUR 3.3 billion of spending needs for maintenance, upgrading and extensions. Adding these resources would increase the budget by a bit less than 50% (OECD/ITF, 2013).

Figure 1.3. **Average annual infrastructure investment requirements in OECD countries to 2025/30**

Source: OECD (2007a), *Infrastructure to 2030 (Vol.2): Mapping Policy for Electricity, Water and Transport*, http://dx.doi.org/10.1787/9789264031326-en.

Figure 1.4. **Quality of infrastructure in G7 economies**

(Scale 1-7; higher score indicates better infrastructure)

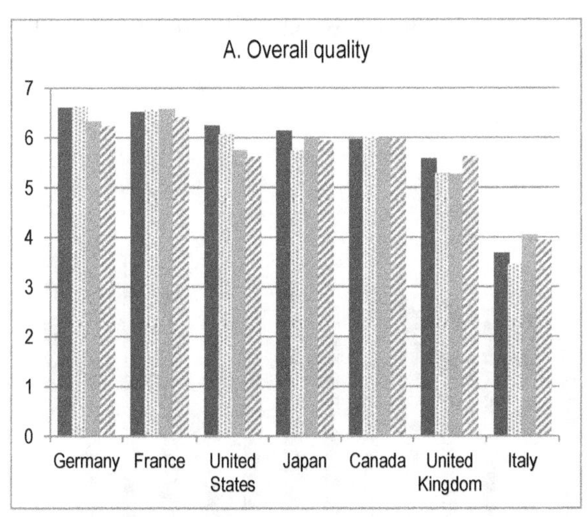

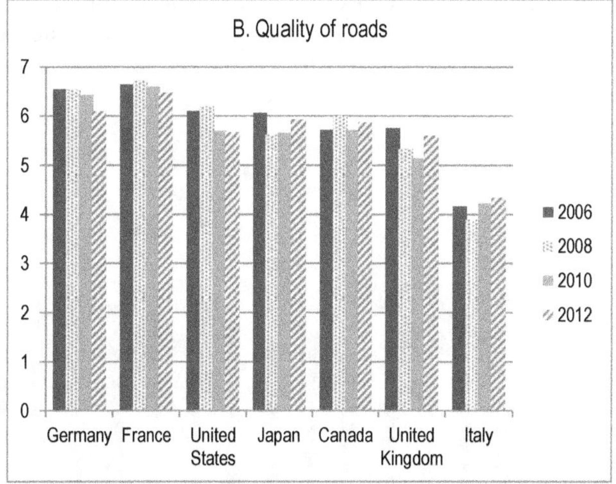

Source: IMF (International Monetary Fund) (2014), "Is it time for an infrastructure push? The macroeconomic effects of public investment", in *World Economic Outlook: Legacies, Clouds, Uncertainties*, IMF, Washington, DC, www.imf.org/external/pubs/ft/weo/2014/02/pdf/c3.pdf.

Avoiding the capture by special interests is essential to maximising the benefits

While there is strong evidence of the need for infrastructure, simply increasing the amount of public spending in infrastructure is not necessarily the solution; it must be productive spending in order to create real economic and social value and utility. The marginal productivity return of infrastructure investment spending, for example, depends on the level of pre-existing infrastructure availability. After surpassing certain thresholds of infrastructure levels, the marginal productivity return declines (UNCTAD, 2009). Thus the decision whether or not to invest in more infrastructure, which infrastructure to invest in and how to invest should be based on a sound needs assessment and cost benefit analysis. Influence by vested interests in the decision may even result in negative return of productivity or excessive infrastructure, creating "white elephant" projects (a project that fails to meet public demand and whose costs of construction, operation and maintenance are not justified by its ultimate utility).

The costs of inefficient spending on public infrastructure are not only economic. Evidence of waste of public resources can cost governments dearly in terms of lost credibility and trust on the part of citizens. Governments are entrusted with spending taxpayers' money efficiently and allocating it for economic and social welfare. Given the increasingly tight fiscal space faced by many governments following the economic crisis, infrastructure spending decisions that are not based on strict needs assessment and cost-benefit analysis could harm not only governments' budgets, but also the confidence of citizens in public institutions.

Transparency International's Global Corruption Barometer 2013, for instance, showed that on average, more than 50% of respondents in OECD countries think that the government is run by a few entities acting in their own interests (Figure 1.5). Corruption is a main obstacle to ensuring effective and efficient investment in public infrastructure. Several studies have shown that "countries with high levels of corruption tend to invest less in education and health systems and more in prestigious infrastructure projects that do not always have obvious benefits for society" (Vargas and Sommer, 2014).

Figure 1.5. **Percentage of respondents who think the government is run by a few big entities acting in their own best interests**

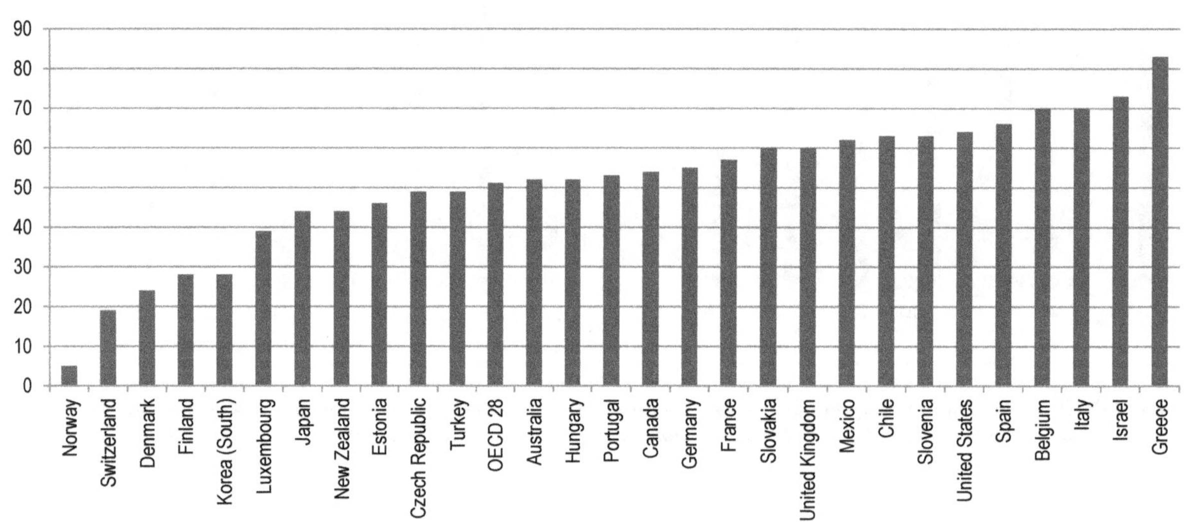

Note: The statistical data for Israel are supplied by and under the responsibility of the relevant Israeli authorities. The use of such data by the OECD is without prejudice to the status of the Golan Heights, East Jerusalem and Israeli settlements in the West Bank under the terms of international law.

Source: Transparency International (2013), "Global Corruption Barometer 2013", www.transparency.org/gcb2013.

The nature of public investment in infrastructure makes it particularly prone to corruption

Bribery, policy capture, embezzlement, abuse of functions, and trading in influence are common examples of corrupt acts, although the exact legal definitions of these vary across countries. Corruption has been identified as one of the most problematic issues with regard to doing business in several OECD countries and it remains a major constraint, dominating the investment climate (WEF, 2014). Within Europe, corruption alone is estimated to cost the EU economy EUR 120 billion per year, just a little less than the annual budget of the European Union (European Commission, 2014). Furthermore, a 2012 Gallup World Poll shows that 57% of the citizens of OECD member countries perceive corruption to be widespread in business.

Recent evidence from the OECD's Foreign Bribery Report suggests that some sectors may be more prone to corruption than others. The report found **that almost 60% of foreign bribery cases occurred in four sectors related to infrastructure**: 19% occurred in the extractives sector, construction (15%), transport and storage (15%) and information and communication (10%). (Figure 1.6)

Figure 1.6. **Sectors where more cases of foreign bribery occurred and the purpose of those bribes, 2014**

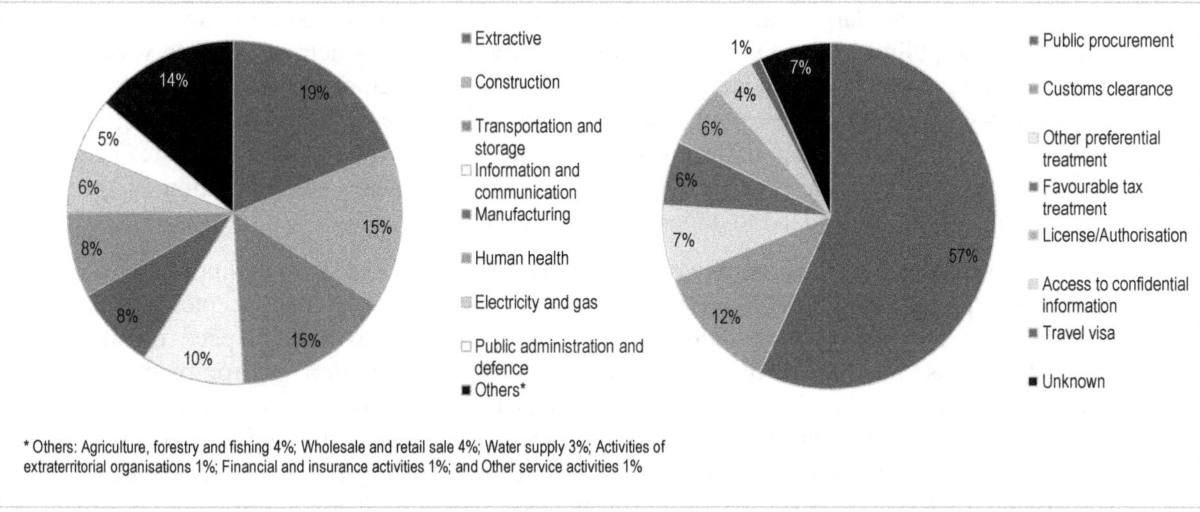

Note: Actors are identified with reference to the United Nations International Standard Industrial Classification of All Economic Activities (UN ISIC), Rev.4 (http://unstats.un.org/unsd/cr/registry/regcst.asp?Cl=27&Lg=1).

Source: OECD (2014b), *OECD Foreign Bribery Report: An Analysis of the Crime of Bribery of Foreign Public Officials*, OECD Publishing, Paris. http://dx.doi.org/10.1787/9789264226616-en.

Corruption allegations concerning government-financed infrastructure projects are common. Indeed, the extent of public officials' discretion over the investment decision, the large sums of money involved, and the multiple stages and stakeholders implicated contribute to making them more vulnerable to undue influence. The potentially adverse effects of the capture of investment decisions by vested interests through low levels of transparency and integrity in lobbying practices and unbalanced financing of political parties are significant. Integrity weaknesses in the procurement process undertaken for administering public infrastructure investment also provide opportunities for corruption. In fact, according to the *OECD Foreign Bribery Report*, in the majority of the cases bribes are paid in order to obtain public procurement contracts (Figure 1.6) (OECD, 2014b). In addition to bribery, bid-rigging, price-gouging, circumvention of the procurement process, fraudulent billing and the delivery of sub-par quality outputs in order to cut costs are amongst the most common corrupt activities concerning the implementation of infrastructure projects. Moreover, as specific investments are increasingly complex in terms of new technologies and computerisation, corruption can occur in the maintenance and after-sale phase, with wrongdoings related to service contracts for maintenance, inspections and upgrades.

The decentralised nature of most public investment projects (see Figure 1.2) may also make them especially open to corrupt practices. On the one hand, decentralisation may narrow the scope for corruption by making politicians more accountable to the citizens they serve (that is, voters should in principle be better able to discern the quality of their leadership and the results they deliver and likewise local politicians should be more in touch with specific needs and contexts of their constituencies). However, there may be a higher risk of corruption at the local level in procurement, due to (in some instances), weaker governance capacity, including less developed local auditing functions, and less visibility to the press and the public (i.e. lower transparency). In many OECD countries, significant corruption risks, notably conflict of interest in decision making, allocation of resources and public procurement, lie at the sub-national level (European Commission, 2014).

Finally, because large-scale infrastructure projects are highly visible to the public, there are also political incentives aligned to such investments, which can lead to waste. For example, politicians may tend to prefer new infrastructure projects rather than maintenance and repairs to existing assets in order to increase their popularity and gain political prestige by having a major infrastructure achievement tied to their mandate. The influence by vested interests at this point is not so much in the administration of the investment, but in the decision to undertake it in the first place.

As an example of unproductive public investment caused by corruption in an investment project, a public official was removed from office for having accepted a bribe estimated to be approximately USD 150 million in relation to a high-speed railway project. It was also found that there had been misappropriation of approximately USD 28.5 million. Following the announcement that the completion date of the railway would be delayed and that the trains would run at a lower speed than initially planned, public concerns over the quality of the transport network have been raised. The cases of corruption involved in this particular project have kept the citizens suspicious of the quality even though the audit service did not find any defect in the quality. After its completion, the low ridership due to high ticket prices has made the service unprofitable, resulting in losses to state revenue.

In another case, allegations of corruption surrounded the publicly funded construction of infrastructures for a major international sporting event. The audit court is investigating fraudulent billing and the relationship between the winning construction company and key public officials. The construction company's donation for the public officials' political party exponentially skyrocketed on the election period before the sporting event. The actual cost of construction is nearly four times as much as what was estimated before the decision was made to host the event. Citizens' discontent was fierce due to the fact that the construction was entirely funded from the public purse, particularly when the country's need for other infrastructure, including energy, water and transportation, is regarded as urgent.

Corruption creates extra burdens and costs on investment, which reduces both quality and value for money

Corruption comes with a high cost. Direct costs include bribe transfers, higher expenses, scarcity of essential services, lower quality and misallocation of public funds (OECD, 2015c). When there are bribe payments involved in the investment process, those paying the bribes can seek to recover the cost of the bribe through inflating prices, billing for work not performed, failing to meet contract standards, reducing quality of work or using inferior materials. This brings about an exaggerated cost of public investment, along with a decrease in the quality of the investment. Evidently, these practices lead to lower investment efficiency. For instance, a study carried out by the OECD and the World Bank highlighted that corruption in both the infrastructure and extractives sectors lead to misallocations of the public budget, which resulted in service delivery that was both low in quality and insufficient in quantity (Table 1.2). Furthermore, recent research has shown that investment, understood largely, only has a positive effect on growth in contexts where corruption is low, whereas its impact in corrupt settings seems insignificant (Dort, Méon and Sekkat, 2014).

Table 1.2. **Consequences of corruption across sectors**

	Infrastructure	Extractives
Misallocation of state revenues	Over-investment and mis-investment in infrastructure facilities.	Budget skewed away from services for the poor. Resource dependency common.
Wasted resources	Too-expensive subsidies. Over-inflated costs in construction cause losses for taxpayers.	Illicit financial flows may reflect stolen state revenues. Inefficient sector governance hampers production and revenue potential.
Inflated prices	Bribes demanded for access to water and electricity. More expensive power supply.	Framework conditions for industrial development in other sectors of the economy largely neglected, resulting in uncompetitive prices for individuals and firms.
Reduced quality	Low-quality roads and other constructions. Poorer utility service provisions (like power cuts).	Few consequences if services are inferior. Lower quality of basic service delivery, including health and education.
Scarcity	Network services not necessarily provided to all districts, despite contractual commitments.	"Scarcity" of competitors if tenders for oil licenses are manipulated.
Unfair allocation of benefits	Poor segments more exposed if there is government failure behind the provision of electricity, water and sanitation.	Political corruption causes income inequalities.
Environment, health and safety	Low quality construction and use of poor or toxic materials damages health, causes invalidity and claims lives. Contamination of water supply, food chain and sanitary systems.	Environmental damage, lack of safety in production (causes health damage and deaths). Contamination of water supply, food chain and sanitary systems.
Other negative consequences	Tax/accounting-related fraud. Theft of electricity supply. Embezzlement in construction.	Conflict/civil war, terror attacks, bunkering (stolen oil), illegal mining.

Source: Based on: OECD (2015c), *Consequences of Corruption at the Sector Level and Implications for Economic Growth and Development*, OECD Publishing, Paris, http://dx.doi.org/10.1787/9789264230781-en.

In addition, corruption also incurs more subtle indirect costs, "such as lower incentives to innovate if market opportunities or jobs are allocated on other grounds than qualifications, the effect of not receiving the government services one is entitled to, lower trust in government institutions, adverse selection of contractors (while honest players stay away), and talented youth placing efforts in rent-seeking/positioning instead of productive labour" (OECD, 2015c). The indirect costs are difficult to quantify and assess, but their potential detrimental effects on the economy, society and the government cannot be ignored.

Assessing the scale of corruption in public infrastructure investment is a challenge because corruption usually leaves no paper trail. However, several studies have estimated the amount of money lost due to corruption. It has been estimated, for example, that between 10-30% of the investment in a publicly funded construction project may be lost through mismanagement and corruption (CoST, 2012). According to another estimation, "annual losses in global construction through mismanagement, inefficiency and corruption could reach USD 2.5 trillion by 2020" (CoST, 2012). Box 1.1 highlights some efforts to estimate the costs of corruption in public infrastructure.

Box 1.1. **Corruption in public infrastructure costs in Canada, China and the Netherlands**

Canada

On 19 October 2011, the Commission of Inquiry on the Awarding and Management of Public Contracts in the Construction Industry, known as the Charbonneau Commission, was established by the Government of Quebec to investigate the scale of collusion and corruption on public construction contracts including, in particular, organisations and businesses of the Government of Quebec and the municipalities, including possible links with political party financing.

Witnesses described different practices in connection with the award of public contracts involving officials, consulting engineering firms, building contractors and political organisations in the municipal and provincial level, such as:

- market allocations schemes
- undue payment of a percentage of the value of contracts awarded in certain municipalities to public officials
- collusion between some engineers and contractors
- corruption of some officials in the municipal and provincial level
- presence of organised crime in the construction industry
- the financing of political parties in connection with the award of public contracts in the construction industry
- use of false invoicing.

China

While the 2008 earthquake in Sichuan, a south-western Chinese province, was certainly a natural phenomenon, much of the destruction and many of the deaths could have been avoided. Of the 70 000 killed, a large number were students who died as school buildings collapsed.

Box 1.1. **Corruption in public infrastructure costs in Canada, China and the Netherlands** *(continued)*

In many cases, relatively new schools were flattened in a matter of seconds, making it impossible for children to escape. By contrast, the surrounding buildings were often still standing, indicating serious structural problems in school construction. Angry parents denounced the schools as substandard "Tofu" projects - that is, as soft as Chinese bean curd - in which local officials and businessmen siphoned off public money.

Four months after the event, a Chinese government committee admitted that shoddy workmanship and substandard materials - allegedly the result of corrupt collusion between officials from the Ministry of Education, local officials and construction companies, who were said pocketing the surplus money - might have been behind the collapse of 7 000 school classrooms.

The Netherlands

On December 2002, following a television documentary providing evidence of collusive behaviour, bid rigging and corrupt practices among construction companies and public officials, several investigations were carried out by the Parliament, the Cabinet, the Department of Justice, and the Dutch Competition Authority. It was found that there was a widespread use of cartels and structural bid rigging within the Dutch construction industry. The media suggested that these malpractices robbed taxpayers of about EUR 0.5 billion each year in approximately 3 500 projects. The investigations and allegations have had a major impact on trust, and the relationship between public sector clients and the construction industry.

Sources: Commission d'enquête sur l'octroi et la gestion des contrats publics dans l'industrie de la construction (2014), "Discours de cloture", www.ceic.gouv.qc.ca/la-commission/discours-de-cloture.html; Dorée, A. G. (2002), "Collusion in the Dutch construction industry: An industrial organization perspective", *Building Research and Information* (2004), 32(2), March–April, pp. 146–156; Wong, Edward (2008), "China admits building flaws in quake", *The New York Times*, September 4, 2008, www.nytimes.com/2008/09/05/world/asia/05china.html?_r=0; Divjak, Carrol (2008), "Corruption and shoddy construction behind school collapses in China earthquake", *World Socialist Web Site*, www.wsws.org/en/articles/2008/10/chin-o16.html.

Corruption in public infrastructure investment also costs governments in lost trust

The costs of fraud and corruption in public investment are not only economic, but also institutional and political, with serious implications for the legitimacy of the state apparatus and the ability of elected leaders and government institutions to function effectively. Figure 1.7 demonstrates the strong relationship between perceived corruption and confidence in national governments. The greater the government corruption is perceived, the lower the confidence.

Figure 1.7. **Correlation: confidence in national government and perception of government corruption, 2014**

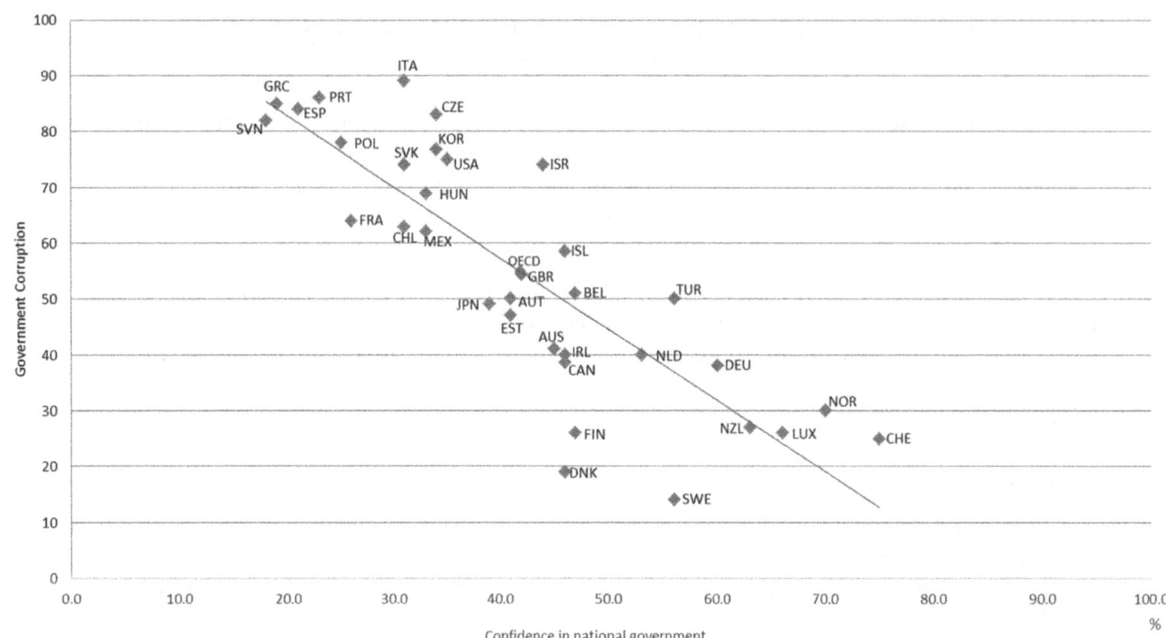

Note: The statistical data for Israel are supplied by and under the responsibility of the relevant Israeli authorities. The use of such data by the OECD is without prejudice to the status of the Golan Heights, East Jerusalem and Israeli settlements in the West Bank under the terms of international law.

Source: Gallup World Poll, www.gallup.com

Given their significant financial and policy implications, large-scale public investment projects are generally highly visible and of great interest to citizens and the media. Poor outcomes or allegations of corruption (although subject to exaggeration from the bandwagon effect) therefore have the potential to influence citizens' views of elected leaders and the effectiveness and legitimacy of public institutions.

Towards a comprehensive, coherent and focused policy framework to promote integrity in public investment

Corruption in the different phases of the public investment cycle, especially infrastructure, can involve a wide range of actors, including elected and non-elected public officials, lobbyists, non-profit organisations, trade unions, contractors, engineers and suppliers. Moreover, given the scale and complexity of infrastructure projects, public officials often rely on consultancy firms for technical assistance. The latter can play a significant role to deter corruption, but their position also provides them with opportunities for corrupt practices. Research shows that consultants can have a strong incentive to prolong the life of projects (Flyvbjerg, Garbuio and Lovallo, 2009), be they feasible or not, as a way to make profits and maintain their network.

The public investment cycle is concerned with corruption in all its forms. It can take place in a variety of ways at different phases, such as undue influence or capture of the investment project by specific interests, or bribery in the procurement process. The following sections identify entry points for corruption and major forms of corrupt practices that take place during the different phases of the public investment cycle. (Figure 1.8)

Figure 1.8. **Public investment cycle**

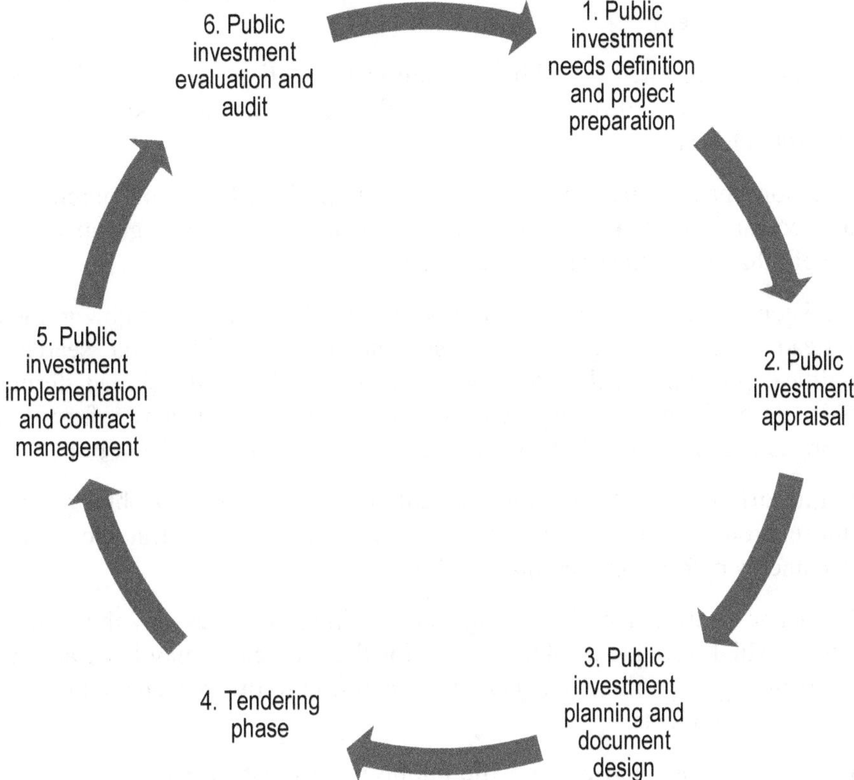

Source: Author's own work.

However, there is no comprehensive, coherent and focused policy framework to address the specific risks of corruption in public investment. Curbing corruption cannot be addressed by policy makers alone – anti-corruption efforts by the business community are also an essential part of the anti-corruption mix. Building on OECD instruments in this area, this section maps out conducts and risks of corruption at each phase of the investment cycle and identifies tools and mechanisms to promote integrity public investment for sustainable economic growth.

1. Needs definition and project preparation phase

The public investment cycle starts with the definition of the needs and the identification of the best way to respond to this need. For example, in the case of a need to cross a river, the needs assessment phase would have to determine whether building a bridge or setting up a ferry line would be the most suitable solution. The needs assessment should ensure that the planned infrastructure or the investment made is economically and socially justified.

The parties involved in the public investment needs and project preparation phase may include high-level elected and non-elected public officials responsible for defining the project, lobbyists, trade unions, regulators, non-governmental organisations (NGOs) and potential contractors. This initial stage of the project cycle is particularly sensitive as policy capture can take place. Moreover, failures here can create fertile ground for corruption at later stages of the project cycle. For instance, it can occur where one or more of these groups seek to undertake a public investment primarily for their own private profit or political benefit and use corrupt practices to achieve this. This may occur, for example, where:

- Interest groups such as lobbyists, political coalitions and/or trade unions use unethical and/or corrupt tactics to influence decision makers towards their specific interest.
- Decision makers are influenced to adopt an investment or purchase that is unnecessary. Such a decision is taken so that a particular group can make a benefit that is of little or no value to society.
- Decision makers are influenced to vote for the development of new infrastructure instead of maintaining existing ones. The reason could be the search for the political prestige attached to new infrastructure being developed during one's mandate or the promise of financial gain, as contracts for new infrastructure are more expensive than maintenance, thus more prone to significant bribes.
- Public officials are bribed by a potential interest group to obtain confidential information on the government policy priorities or strategic government documents before these are made public.
- Exchanges between project designers and intermediaries, involving the public bodies which provide or obtain funds for the project(s), may have an impact on the planning of public works *per se* and can lead to the introduction of inaccurate policy requirements.
- Elected officials choose a specific public investment to benefit contractors who contributed to his/her political campaign.
- Elected officials favour public investment that will be carried out through concessions or public-private partnerships (PPPs) to benefit a private operator who contributed to their political campaigns.
- A specific public investment is selected because the public official responsible for approving the public investment has received a bribe from a potential contractor.
- A specific public investment is selected because the public official or his/her family member is part of the board of the potential company developing, building or participating in the construction of the public investment.
- A specific public investment is selected because the public official has allegiance (previous employment or business relationships) with the potential company developing, building or participating in the construction of the public investment.

2. Appraisal phase

The appraisal phase serves to evaluate an infrastructure project's feasibility, to give the official approval and to determine how and by whom it will be financed. Banks, private firms, pension funds and insurance companies play an important role in providing resources to undertake public investment projects, but the appraisal phase also concerns the release of public funds that would need the approval of certain public entities. Consultants are often hired to undertake feasibility studies and cost/benefit analyses.

During this phase, elected and non-elected public officials at all levels of government, companies, consultants, lobbyists and financial stakeholders (banks, financial agents) can corruptly seek and/or manage a financing arrangement for the public investment. This may occur, for example, where:

- A consultancy firm in charge of the feasibility study intentionally provides an under-estimation of the costs while overestimating the benefits.
- Consultants prolong the life of projects as a way to make profits and maintain their networks.
- A public official presents incomplete or false information regarding the social, economic and/or environmental feasibility studies to ensure the public investment is approved.
- A public official or the intended contractor/private operator bribes the person (or firm) carrying out the social, economic and/or environmental feasibility studies to ensure the public investment is approved.
- The investor's financial risk assessments may be negated or manipulated to downplay the risks associated with the contractor. The potential private operator of a PPP or a concession bribes a public official to not carry out a proper risk allocation, sensitivity analysis or other guarantee measures. This allows increasing the amount paid by the government to financially balance the project at the start or during future renegotiations.
- The potential private operator of a PPP or a concession bribes a public official for him not to secure the land where the project will be carried out and to disclose information about the location so the potential private operator of a PPP or a concession can buy the land and increase the price of expropriation.
- A financial institution or agent, such as a bank, pays a bribe to a public official in charge of the public investment in return for the institution or agent being awarded the contract to finance the investment.

3. Planning and document design phase

The development of the bidding documents and terms of references is a very important step for the clean and fair management of the infrastructure project as it determines the specificities and details of the work to be undertaken. These documents must ensure that a competitive bidding process and a trustworthy cost-benefit analysis are the basis on which the contractor(s) will be selected. It is essential that the bidding documents and terms of reference are made available to all possible candidates to ensure that all are on an equal footing. In addition, procurement announcements should be made sufficiently in advance to guarantee an adequate timeframe for bidders to express their interest.

The parties involved in the planning and document design phases include the project owner(s), public officials responsible for issuing planning permits and other approvals and potential bidders and contractors. The following are examples of corrupt practices during the planning and design phase of a project:

- Needed goods, services or maintenance costs are over- or under-estimated to favour a particular potential bidder.
- Hidden mistakes and fictitious positions can be built into the project calculation and design, affecting the terms of reference, which leaves openings that can later be used to conveniently account for increased costs, influence the selection process or the selection procedure. For instance, partners may decide to:
  - limit the timeframe for the tendering process
  - use specifications that preclude competitive bidding
  - select additional fictitious bidders or ones unlikely to submit competitive bids
  - plan a very low bid price and include "hidden" possibilities to expand the contract at a later stage to recover the economies for the supplier.
- The terms of reference are developed so as to be excessively confusing in order to hide manipulations and corruption and to make monitoring difficult.
- The contractor bribes a public official in order to obtain planning permits for the public investment, or to obtain approval for a design that does not meet relevant building regulations.
- Companies bribe a public official or local authority to obtain confidential information about the planning and design process.
- Potential bidders collude to ensure that the design of the tender will only favour one of the bidders (cartels).
- A company bribes public officials or the authority responsible for the design of the public investment to tailor the design for him/her and disqualify other potential bidders. For example, a certain technology only possessed by one of the bidders may be specified, even though other technologies may be preferable or less costly.
- A company bribes decision makers to favour a direct "emergency" contract, circumventing open competition.
- The design firm, architect or engineer has a close relationship with the public official in charge of the public investment (e.g. family or former colleagues), the contractor or the consultants.
- The tender is artificially split into several lots, in order to stay below certain procedural thresholds.
- Estimates for the infrastructure works are kept low, in order to shift important expenses to the maintenance and after-sale phase. In this way the investment is more likely to take place, and the most important gains go to the maintenance contractor.

4. Tendering phase

The tendering phase is when bids are evaluated and contractor(s) selected based on their technical and cost proposal. The project owner can choose to contract directly with a main construction contractor and with consulting engineers. Alternatively, the project owner can leave the whole project to a managing contractor or enter into a contract agreement with several different contractors for different packages (GIACC, 2013). The criteria for selection need to be clear and transparent; the decision needs to be unbiased and the officials in charge should not have any conflict of interest with the bidders. Therefore, the submitted documents remain confidential until the decision has been made, to avoid the manipulation of prices and that the contracting authority has a clear idea of the market, costs and prices to develop an appropriate cost estimation.

In this phase, the main actors are the bidders, contractors and public officials. This phase is particularly vulnerable to corruption. The following examples reflect how corruption may occur when awarding a public procurement contract or a public-private partnership:

- Bidders bribe a public official or the consultant engineer to obtain confidential information about the process, the tender documents and the reference price, resulting in asymmetry of information for all potential bidders.
- A bidder bribes the public official in charge of the public investment in order to reject another properly qualified bidder at the pre-qualification stage.
- The bidder bribes a public official, in return for which the public official ensures that the bribing bidder wins the contract. For example, the public official manipulates the tender evaluation, such as the points given on the technical evaluation, thus ensuring that the bribing tenderer wins.
- The official ensures that there is no competitive process. The public official may announce false reasons for a direct award (e.g. special technology possessed only by the tenderer, emergency, or national security).
- The bidder provides a contribution to the ruling party to ensure that he/she will obtain the procurement contract or the concession without competition or that the evaluation method will benefit him/her only. Bidders collude to give the appearance of competition through bid-rigging schemes such as cover bidding, bid suppression, bid rotation and market allocation.
- The public official awards contracts to companies owned by his/her family members or to companies with which he/she has a relationship (e.g. previous or future employer).

5. Implementation and contract execution phase

The contract execution phase involves the project owner, the architect, consulting engineers, contractors, suppliers, and their respective sub-contractors (GIACC, 2013). This phase is the most concrete insofar as the actual construction or maintenance work takes place in this segment of the cycle. It starts by the finalisation of the contract and the conclusion of the financial agreements, and ends when the contract expires. This phase implies the attribution of management responsibility to ensure proper management of works and outputs and responsibility lines. It is important that a consensual dispute resolution mechanism is agreed upon to manage any potential disagreements and conflicts. The concretisation of the selected proposal brings about many new decisions related to the supplied material, the timetable, labour arrangements and any other possible unexpected event that might change the initial agreement.

Even though they are rarely covered by procurement regulations, the steps following the evaluation and actual contract award are as vulnerable to corruption as the previous phases of the procurement cycle, and it is essential to have a mechanism in place to ensure the contract is implemented properly, without changes in costs or level of quality. The following examples reflect how corruption may occur when implementing and executing a contract:

- The contractor has many ways to defraud the public budget: rendering of fictitious work, inflating the work volume, changing orders, using lower quality materials than specified in the contract, supplying goods of a lower price and quality than quoted, rendering contracted services in an improper way, etc.
- Renegotiations of the contract and terms of references is allowed after the contract was awarded, changing the initial requirements.
- The contractor bribes the public official and/or the consultant engineer to allow "change orders", modifications to the public investment increasing the scope, time and costs, resulting in higher prices paid by the government.
- The contractor bribes the public official and/or the consultant engineer to approve defective or non-existent work.
- The contractor provides false invoices and bribes the public official and/or the consultant engineer to approve or overlook the discrepancy.
- The contractor misprices the goods or services and bribes the public official and/or the consultant engineer to approve or overlook the discrepancy.
- The contractor does false reporting of work time and qualification of his/her staff to increase or justify the cost paid by the government and bribes the public official and/or the consultant engineer to not verify the validity of the reporting.

6. Evaluation and audit phase

The crucial and final phase of the infrastructure project is the monitoring and evaluation phase, whereby internal control mechanisms are applied by relevant ministries. Credible and independent internal and external audits that can verify the application of said controls as well as audit public works projects directly must exist. The reviewing body needs to be independent from the public entity that initiated the procurement process. The institutional evaluation framework as well as the analytical evaluation framework should be decided from the start and appear in the contract to ensure that the right information is gathered throughout the entirety of the contract execution (EPEC, 2015).

During this phase, contractors, evaluators and public officials can misrepresent activities and results through: *i)* discrepancies in financial reporting; *ii)* non-compliance with financial or non-financial standards and terms; and *iii)* substandard performance. The following examples reflect how corruption may manifest in these ways:

- Auditors are bribed to overlook faults in financial risk assessments by the contracting entity that would otherwise point to risks in awarding the contract to the winning bid.
- A stakeholder falsifies information about the financing, processes and/or results in order to have falsely positive evaluations.
- Stakeholders forge financial documentation requested by the auditors.

- Information is purposely not publicly disclosed in order to avoid evaluation by civil society.
- Internal or external auditors are complicit in limiting the information it requests as part of the audit execution.
- Actors are complicit in fragmenting contracts to avoid meeting the financial threshold that requires an *ex ante* or *a priori* audit, in order to move ahead with projects that have not been structured in compliance with regulations.
- The public official hires a company with which he has close relationship to ensure that the auditor will not report the findings.
- The contractor and/or the public official bribe the auditor to ensure that the auditor will not report legitimate findings of non-compliance and substandard performance.
- Auditors are bribed to report favourable audit observations.

Bibliography

Ades, A. and R. Di Tella (1999), "Rents, competition and corruption", *American Economic Review* 89(4), pp. 982-993, http://tu-dresden.de/die_tu_dresden/fakultaeten/philosophische_fakultaet/is/makro/lehre/download/rntexte/we/ades%20ti%20tella.pdf.

Anderson, E., P. de Renzio and S. Levy (2006), "The Role of Public Investment in Poverty Reduction: Theories, Evidence and Methods", *Overseas Development Institute*, www.odi.org/sites/odi.org.uk/files/odi-assets/publications-opinion-files/1786.pdf.

Beck, P. and M. Maker (1986), "A comparison of bribery and bidding in thin markets", *Economic Letters*, 20, pp. 1-5.

Bo Dal, E. and M. A. Rossi (2007), "Corruption and inefficiency: Theory and evidence from electric utilities", *Journal of Public Economics,* Elsevier, Vol. 91(5-6), pp. 939-962, June, www.sciencedirect.com/science/article/B6V76-4MWXT56-1/2/775f042ac4bb49feacc304867c4eeddb.

Broudehoux, A.M. (2007), "Spectacular Beijing: The conspicuous construction of an olympic metropolis", *Journal of Urban Affairs*, Volume 29, Issue 4, pp. 383–399, http://onlinelibrary.wiley.com/doi/10.1111/j.1467-9906.2007.00352.x/pdf.

Charron, N. et al. (2012), "Regional Governance Matters: A Study on Regional Variation in Quality of Government within the EU", WP 01/2012, Directorate-General for Regional Policy, Brussels.

Commission d'enquête sur l'octroi et la gestion des contrats publics dans l'industrie de la construction (2014), "Discours de cloture", www.ceic.gouv.qc.ca/la-commission/discours-de-cloture.html.

CoST (Construction Sector Transparency Initiative) (2012), "Openness and accountability in public infrastructure could save $2.5 trillion by 2020", press release, www.constructiontransparency.org/documentdownload.axd?documentresourceid=8.

Cuervo-Cazurra, A. (2008), "The effectiveness of laws against bribery abroad", *Journal of International Business Studies* 39(4), pp. 634-651.

D'Souza, A. (2012), "The OECD Anti-Bribery Convention: Changing the currents of trade," *Journal of Development Economics* 97, pp. 73-87.

Dabla-Norris, E. et al. (2011), "Investing in public investment: An index of public investment efficiency", *IMF Working Paper*, WP/11/37, www.imf.org/external/pubs/ft/wp/2011/wp1137.pdf.

Daehre, K.-H. (2012), "Zukunft der Verkehrsinfrastrukturfinanzierung", Bericht der Kommission, December.

Divjak, C. (2008), "Corruption and shoddy construction behind school collapses in China earthquake", *World Socialist Web Site,* www.wsws.org/en/articles/2008/10/chin-o16.html.

Dorée, A. G. (2002), "Collusion in the Dutch construction industry: An industrial organization perspective", *Building Research and Information* (2004), 32(2), March–April, pp. 146–156.

Dort, T., P-G. Méon and K. Sekkat (2014), "Does investment spur growth everywhere? Not where institutions are weak", *Kyklos*, Volume 67, Issue 4, pp. 482–505, http://onlinelibrary.wiley.com/doi/10.1111/kykl.12064/abstract.

Eccles, R. G., I. Ioannou and G. Serafeim (2011), "The Impact of Corporate Sustainability on Organizational Processes and Performance", *Management Science*, 23 November, http://papers.ssrn.com/sol3/papers.cfm?abstract_id=1964011.

Economic Policy Institute (2012), *Public Investment: The Next 'New Thing' for Powering Economic Growth*, www.epi.org/publication/bp338-public-investments/.

EPEC (European PPP Expertise Centre) (2015), "Procurement notice, prequalification and shortlisting", www.eib.org/epec/g2g/iii-procurement/31/311/index.htm.

European Commission (2014) "Report from the Commission to the Council and the European Parliament - EU Anti-Corruption Report", http://ec.europa.eu/dgs/home-affairs/e-library/documents/policies/organized-crime-and-human-trafficking/corruption/docs/acr_2014_en.pdf.

European Investment Bank (2010), "Public and private financing of infrastructure", *EIB Papers*, Volume 15, No. 1, www.eib.org/attachments/efs/eibpapers/eibpapers_2010_v15_n01_en.pdf.

Flyvbjerg, B., M. Garbuio and D. Lovallo (2009), "Delusion and deception in large infrastructure projects: Two models for explaining and preventing executive disaster". *California Management Review*, Vol. 51, No. 2.

Gestrin, M. (2014), "Investment Insights: International investment in Europe: A canary in the coal mine?", www.oecd.org/daf/inv/investment-policy/InvestmentInsights-Nov2014.pdf.

GIACC (Global Infrastructure Anti-Corruption Centre) (2013), "How corruption occurs", www.giaccentre.org/how_corruption_occurs.php.

Habib, M. and L. Zurawicki (2002), "Corruption and foreign direct investment," *Journal of International Business Studies*, Vol. 33, No. 2 (2nd Qtr.), pp. 291-307.

Hakkala, K. et al. (2008), "Asymmetric effects of corruption on FDI: Evidence from Swedish multinational firms", *Review of Economics and Statistics*, November, 90(4) pp. 627–642, www.mitpressjournals.org/doi/pdf/10.1162/rest.90.4.627.

Haquea, E. and R. Kneller (2008), "Public investment and growth: The role of corruption", Centre for Growth and Business Cycles Research, and Economic Studies, the University of Manchester, www.socialsciences.manchester.ac.uk/medialibrary/cgbcr/discussionpapers/dpcgbcr98.pdf.

Hawkins, J. (2013), "How to note: Reducing corruption in infrastructure sectors", *Evidence on Demand*, www.engineersagainstpoverty.org/documentdownload.axd?documentresourceid=4.

IMF (International Monetary Fund) (2014), "Is it time for an infrastructure push? The macroeconomic effects of public investment", in IMF, *World Economic Outlook: Legacies, Clouds, Uncertainties*, Washington DC, www.imf.org/external/pubs/ft/weo/2014/02/pdf/c3.pdf.

Jensen, N. and J. Malesky (2014), "Does the OECD Anti-Bribery Convention reduce bribery? An empirical analysis using the unmatched count technique", working paper, www.natemjensen.com/wp-content/uploads/2014/09/20141205_OECD_Working-Paper_ejm.pdf.

Jeong, Y. and R.J. Weiner (2012), "Who bribes? Evidence from the United Nations Oil-for-Food Program", *Strategic Management Journal.*

Khwaja, A. I. and A. Mian (2015), "Do lenders favor politically connected firms?", *The Quarterly Journal of Economics* (2005), http://qje.oxfordjournals.org/content/120/4/1371.full.pdf+html.

Lee, S.-H., and D. Weng (2013), "Does bribery in the home country promote or dampen firm exports?", *Strategic Management Journal* 34, pp. 1472-1487, http://199.171.202.195/doi/10.1002/smj.2075/epdf.

Leys, C. (1965), "What is the problem about corruption?" *Journal of Modern African Studies* 3, pp. 215-230, reprint in A.J. Heidenheimer, M. Johnston and V.T. LeVine (eds.), *Political corruption: A Handbook*, pp. 51-66, 1989, Transaction Books, Oxford.

Lim, Guang Eng (2002), "Enforcing accountability by and the transparency of political parties" in *Taking Action against Corruption in Asia and the Pacific*, proceedings of the 3rd Regional Anti-Corruption Conference, Manila, ABD/OECD, www.oecd.org/site/adboecdanti-corruptioninitiative/regionalseminars/35137400.pdf.

Lui, F. (1985), "An equilibrium queuing model of bribery", *Journal of Political Economy*, August, pp. 760-781.

Malesky, E. J., D. D. Gueorguiev and N. M. Jensen (2014), "Monopoly money: Foreign investment and bribery in Vietnam, A survey experiment", *American Journal of Political Science*, http://onlinelibrary.wiley.com/doi/10.1111/ajps.12126/epdf.

Mauro, P. (1996), "The effects of corruption on growth, investment, and government expenditure", *IMF Working Paper*, Vol. 96/98, pp. 1-28, http://ssrn.com/abstract=882994.

Mauro, P. (1995), "Corruption and growth", *The Quarterly Journal of Economics*, August.

McKinsey Global Institute (2013), "Infrastructure productivity: How to save $1 trillion a year", www.mckinsey.com/insights/engineering_construction/infrastructure_productivity.

OECD (2015a), *Government at a Glance 2015*, OECD Publishing, Paris, http://dx.doi.org/10.1787/gov_glance-2015-en.

OECD (2015b), *OECD National Accounts Statistics* (database), http://dx.doi.org/10.1787/na-data-en (accessed on 20 October 2015).

OECD (2015c), *Consequences of Corruption at the Sector Level and Implications for Economic Growth and Development*, OECD Publishing, Paris, http://dx.doi.org/10.1787/9789264230781-en.

OECD (2014a), *OECD Regional Outlook 2014: Regions and Cities: Where Policies and People Meet*, OECD Publishing, Paris, http://dx.doi.org/10.1787/9789264201415-en.

OECD (2014b), *OECD Foreign Bribery Report: An Analysis of the Crime of Bribery of Foreign Public Officials*, OECD Publishing, Paris, http://dx.doi.org/10.1787/9789264226616-en.

OECD (2013), *Government at a Glance 2013*, OECD Publishing, Paris, http://dx.doi.org/10.1787/gov_glance-2013-en.

OECD (2011), *Making the Most of Public Investment in a Tight Fiscal Environment: Multi-level Governance Lessons from the Crisis*, OECD Publishing, Paris, http://dx.doi.org/10.1787/9789264114470-en.

OECD (2007a), *Infrastructure to 2030 (Vol.2): Mapping Policy for Electricity, Water and Transport*, OECD Publishing, Paris, http://dx.doi.org/10.1787/9789264031326-en.

OECD/ITF (International Transport Forum) (2013), *ITF Transport Outlook 2013: Funding Transport*, OECD Publishing/ITF, Paris, http://dx.doi.org/10.1787/9789282103937-en.

PWC (PricewaterhouseCoopers) (2012), "Developing infrastructure in Asia Pacific: Outlook, challenges and solutions", www.pwc.com/sg/en/capital-projects-infrastructure/assets/cpi-develop-infrastructure-in-ap-201405.pdf.

Robertson, C. J. and A. Watson (2004), "Corruption and change: The impact of foreign direct investment", *Strategic Management Journal*, Vol. 25, No. 4, April, pp. 385-396.

Shah, A. (2006a), "Corruption and decentralized public governance", *World Bank Policy Research Working Paper* 3824, January.

Shah, A. (2006b), "Decentralised provision of public infrastructure and corruption", *International Center for Public Policy Working Paper Series* #1418, Andrew Young School of Policy Studies, Georgia State University.

Standard and Poor's (2014), "Global infrastructure: How to fill a $500 billion hole", *Ratings Direct*, January, www.engagedinvestor.co.uk/Journals/2014/01/30/n/a/q/How-To-Fill-A.pdf.

Straub, S. (2008), "Infrastructure and growth in developing countries: Recent advances and research challenges", *Policy Research Working Papers*, The World Bank, http://elibrary.worldbank.org/doi/pdf/10.1596/1813-9450-4460.

Swedish International Development Cooperation Agency (2015), *Sidas hantering av korruptionsmisstankar, årsrapport 2014*, www.sida.se/globalassets/global/sa-arbetar-vi/anti-corruption/sida_arsrapport_2014_korruption_se_webb.pdf.

Tanzi, V and H. Davoodi (2008), *Roads to Nowhere: How Corruption in Public Investment Hurts Growth*, www.imf.org/external/pubs/ft/issues12/issue12.pdf.

Transparency International (2014), *Corruption Perceptions Index 2014*, www.transparency.org/cpi2014.

Transparency International (2013), "Global Corruption Barometer 2013", www.transparency.org/gcb2013.

Tyler Lund, M. (2010), "Foreign direct investment: Catalyst of economic growth", PhD dissertation, http://content.lib.utah.edu/utils/getfile/collection/etd2/id/1969/filename/image.

UK Chartered Institute of Building (2013), "A report exploring corruption in the UK construction sector", http://www.ciob.org/sites/default/files/CIOB%20research%20-%20Corruption%20in%20the%20UK%20Construction%20Industry%20September%202013.pdf.

UN (United Nations) (2009), *World Population to 2300*, www.un.org/esa/population/publications/longrange2/WorldPop2300final.pdf.

UN (2003), "Report of the International Conference on Financing for Development, Monterrey, Mexico, 18-22 March 2002", (A/CONF.198/11, Chapter 1, Resolution 1, Annex), www.un.org/en/events/pastevents/pdfs/MonterreyConsensus.pdf.

UNCTAD (United Nations Conference on Trade and Development) (2009), "The role of public investment in social and economic development", http://unctad.org/en/0Docs/webdiae20091_en.pdf.

Vargas, M. and F. Sommer (2014), "Corruption and the risks of losses on government bonds", *Risk Management*, Edition 3.3.

WEF (World Economic Forum) (2014), *The Global Competitiveness Report 2014-2015*, www3.weforum.org/docs/WEF_GlobalCompetitivenessReport_2014-15.pdf.

Wei, Shang –Jin (2000), "How taxing is corruption on international investors?", *The Review of Economics and Statistics*, February, 82(1), pp. 1–11, http://users.nber.org/~wei/data/wei2000a/wei2000a.pdf.

Wei, Shang –Jin (1997), "Why is corruption so more taxing than tax? Arbitrariness kills", www.nber.org/papers/w6255.pdf.

Wells, J. (2015), "Corruption in the construction of public infrastructure: Critical issues in project preparation", Chr. Michelsen Institute (U4 Issue 2015:8).

Wong, E. (2008), "China Admits Building Flaws in Quake", *The New York Times*, September 4, 2008, www.nytimes.com/2008/09/05/world/asia/05china.html?_r=0.

Woo, Jung-Yeop and Uk Heo (2009), "Corruption and foreign direct investment attractiveness in Asia", *Asian Politics and Policy*, Volume 1, Issue 2, p. 223–238, http://onlinelibrary.wiley.com/doi/10.1111/j.1943-0787.2009.01113.x/pdf.

World Bank (2015), "World Bank Open Data", http://data.worldbank.org/.

World Bank (2005), *A Better Investment Climate for Everyone*, http://siteresources.worldbank.org/INTWDRS/Resources/477365-1327693758977/FNL_WDR_SA_Overview6.pdf.

International surveys measuring confidence and satisfaction with government, institutions and services: Web links

Gallup World Poll: www.gallup.com.

Chapter 2

Framework to promote integrity in public investment

The Integrity Framework for Public Investment provides concrete measures and mechanisms that could be employed at each phase of the public investment cycle in order to safeguard integrity. In addition, this chapter provides more than 40 examples of good implementation measures and mechanisms already existing in the public and private sectors.

Following the mapping of conducts and risks of corruption at each phase of the investment cycle, this chapter will suggest measures and tools to prevent corruption, mitigate the risks, and to redress them by addressing each of the conducts and risks previously identified. The following table presents a framework of policy objectives and options to adequately promote integrity in public investment.

Table 2.1. **Integrity Framework for Public Investment**

Phase	Policy objective	Policy options
Applicable to all phases of the public investment cycle	Providing standards of conduct of elected and non-elected public officials	• Developing codes of conduct, which include: ➢ clear mission of the organisation, its values and principles ➢ clear definitions on what constitutes a corruption risk ➢ guidelines on how public servants deal with ethical dilemmas, prejudices and grey areas that are encountered in everyday work ➢ sanctions for integrity breaches. • Raising awareness and capacity on standards of conduct through training on the code of conduct, values and principles. • Defining public officials in "at risk" areas with specific codes of conduct, especially for those who have higher interaction with private sector.
	Identifying and managing conflict-of-interest situations	• Developing conflict-of-interest and private-interest disclosure provisions (OECD 2003 Guidelines for Managing Conflict of Interests in the Public Service). • Providing clear examples and situations of private interests that may lead to potential conflict of interest situations. • Setting specific restrictions and prohibitions on public officials (especially in decision-making positions) working in the public procurement authority or responsible for public procurement in government bodies. • Requiring public officials to disclose their family members' private interests where potential conflicts of interest may arise.
	Providing standards of conduct for the private sector and consultants	• Ensuring that the public sector develops and implements codes of conduct for private sector employees, which include: ➢ clear examples of activities that will compromise the ethical behaviour of the business when working closely with the public sector ➢ punishments for integrity breaches including administrative, disciplinary and criminal breaches. • Applying strong legal sanctions to contractors who offer bribe payments such as restrictions on participation in future investment projects or other public procurement processes. • Ensuring support and commitment from senior management in the prevention of corruption in public investment.
	Regulating and limiting the use of confidential information by public officials	• Cancelling retrospectively the decisions based on confidential information. • Setting up mechanisms that prevent confidential information, authority or influence from being used for personal gain or for improper advantage of other businesses and non-profit organisations.
	Providing protection for employees who report wrongdoings or breaches of integrity in both the private and public sector	• Providing consistent advice and support to staff in case of questions or having witnessed misconduct and integrity breaches through a whistleblower hotline. • Developing guidelines to report wrongdoing in case of integrity breaches or mismanagement. • Providing effective protection ensuring that private and public sector employees, as well as their careers, are protected, in case they report wrongdoing in good faith.

Phase	Policy objective	Policy options
Needs definition and selection phase	Ensuring that public investment decisions are based on national, regional or sectorial objectives	• Providing online platforms where the public is invited to inform national infrastructure priorities. • Setting up an independent body responsible for assessing the national infrastructure needs. • Co-ordinate with sub-national governments to ensure that strategic priorities for investment are well aligned across levels of government.
	Ensuring that the selection of public investment projects does not favour a particular interest group or individual over the public interest	• Rendering the decision-making process more transparent by: ➢ Making relevant information available publicly through channels such as websites and newsletters. ➢ Ensuring that this information reaches civil society and the media, who play a particular role in keeping stakeholders accountable. ➢ Publishing information and reports regarding long-term national and development plans. • Increasing citizen participation through: ➢ participatory budgets. ➢ websites for citizens to prioritise public investments. • Inviting relevant groups to participate in the decision-making process: ➢ finding the right mix of participants and ensuring that no group is inadvertently excluded. ➢ carrying out stakeholder mapping and analysis. ➢ consulting experts and "outsiders" from the public administration to evaluate the pertinence of the public investment, and publicly disclosing the results of that consultation. • Securing transparency and integrity in lobbying (OECD 2010 Principles on Transparency and Integrity in Lobbying) by: ➢ introducing a lobbying registry. ➢ implementing regulations of revolving doors (e.g. cooling-off period, etc.). ➢ ensuring transparency/balanced composition in advisory group.
	Preventing elected officials from choosing a specific public investment to benefit contractors who contributed to their political campaign	• Banning certain types of private contributions, in particular: ➢ corporations with government contracts or partial government ownership. ➢ corporate donations, trade unions, etc. ➢ foreign corporate donations. • Introducing a limit for private funding. • Requiring disclosures of information regarding political funding and ensuring that: ➢ information is timely, reliable, accessible and intelligible; public disclosure of reports. ➢ information is complete and includes private donations. • Promoting media and civil society scrutiny. • Ensuring that companies/contractors publish their contributions to political campaigns and political parties on line. • Ensuring independent and efficient oversight by: ➢ strengthening independence of monitoring body and process. ➢ providing capacity through sufficient resources and specialised auditing capacities and methodologies. • Providing for dissuasive and enforceable sanctions in the case of breaches.

Phase	Policy objective	Policy options
Appraisal phase	Ensuring that the awarding of the contract to banks to finance the investment is based on cost and their capacity to finance, and that it is not inflicted by other undue influence	• Bankers following codes of conduct with specific regulations requiring more scrutiny for those having higher interaction with the public sector. • Implementing legislations or codes of conduct that explicitly prohibit public officials from receiving certain payments or gifts that may create conflict-of-interest situations to their official duty. • Demanding higher scrutiny for senior officials who have more discretion and decision-making power.
	Ensuring objectivity and credibility of social, economic and environmental feasibility studies	• Limiting discretionary scope of public officials in the assessment through: ➢ delegating the assessment studies to external experts for social, economic and environmental feasibility studies or ➢ providing public officials with standardised assessment guidelines. • If a consultancy firm is to assess the feasibility of the project, a due diligence check should be carried out prior to the selection and the selection should be the result of a fair and transparent procurement process. • Publishing the studies for which the public officials or the experts who carried out the studies will be held responsible. • Assuring a proper public consultation process associated with the relevant feasibility studies. • Keeping record of the assessment of the expert on their report for future reference and penalising those with alleged bias on future public investment project assessments. • Restricting room for undue influence on the experts through: ➢ sanctions on public officials who try to unduly influence the experts' studies ➢ carrying out internal concomitant audit and having external scrutiny.
	Limiting the influence of a potential private operator of a public-private partnership (PPP) or a concession	• Establishing standards for risk analysis that limit the room for public officials' discretion. • Publishing the studies and holding the persons who carried out the report responsible. • Concomitant, or real-time, audit. • Providing regulations and sanctions on the use of confidential information by public officials in legislation or in codes of conduct.
Planning and document design phase	Limiting the possibility of actors getting more information as an improper favour	• Digitalising information dissemination. • Establishing sound and comprehensive e-procurement systems for the complete dissemination of public procurement information.
	Ensuring that the design of the tender documents and specifications are not restrictive or tailored	• Creating an independent assessor commission/committee that will address bidders' concerns regarding the design of the tender. • Establishing a tender template limiting over-specification. • Involving experts groups or individuals to participate/help in the design of the tender documents and specifications to avoid restrictive specifications. • Ensuring that designs are complete and a technical commission undertakes site surveys.

Phase	Policy objective	Policy options
Tendering phase	Ensuring that the winning bidder is the most qualified	• Use of integrity pacts so that the government officials and companies adhere to an ethical conduct during the procurement process. • Implementing an Integrity Framework. • Providing verbal debriefing by the government to aggrieved bidders to provide a better understanding of how the decision was reached, increasing understanding of the integrity involved in the process. • Inviting civil society to monitor that the process is carried out in a transparent manner (e.g. use of social witnesses). • Ensuring that a review and remedy system is in place that has the following characteristics: ➢ providing timely redress ➢ being effective in correcting (and thus preventing) instances of unlawfulness on the part of economic operators and/or contracting authorities ➢ being transparent and clear (i.e. understandable and easy to use by economic operators) ➢ being non-discriminatory and available to all the bidders wishing to participate in a specific contract award procedure. • Carrying out a parallel independent procurement evaluation to strengthen the detection of collusion, bid-rigging and favouring a supplier.
	Assuring the integrity of bidding companies	• Requiring all bidders on a contract to produce independent certification as a pre-qualification requirement, or specifying the necessity to comply with certain standards to participate in the bidding process.
	Preventing bid rigging, collusion or the agree sharing of the market or future contracts in a public investment	• Using framework agreements created through competitive processes. • Using a pre-qualification system with the adequate technical, financial and qualitative criteria. The pre-qualification phase could include a background check on previous corruption offenses. • Using a two-envelope approach whereby the envelope containing the price is only considered following a technical evaluation.
	Ensuring that non-competitive procedures are not used without proper justification	• Clearly defining and disseminating legal requirements for the use of a non-competitive procedure. • Ensuring that all the justifications are properly presented and make them public. • Ensuring that this type of decision is not at the discretion of one individual. (e.g. Four-eyes Principle).
Implementation and contract management phase	Ensuring that there is not false reporting of invoices regarding costs associated to materials, labour hours and the qualifications of staff	• Publicising the estimated cost of the project and the final cost incurred to citizens through media and community groups. • Ensuring that profit and labour costs are separated from the rates for materials and equipment. • Increasing the functionalities of the e-procurement systems to cover the contract management phase and assure publication of relevant information in informational portals, including variations and reasons for the overrun.

Phase	Policy objective	Policy options
	Ensuring that there is no delay in public investment due to corrupt practices	• Creating a website that monitors in real time the advancement of the public investment and how the advancement compares to the cost and time estimations. • Training community monitors to observe the progress and quality of the project.
Evaluation and audit phase	Ensuring that the entities (public or private) have an effective system of internal controls and financial reporting to monitor and identify irregularities.	• Application of the Committee of Sponsoring Organizations of the Treadway Commission (COSO) Framework on internal control. In particular, a few requirements stand out: ➢ There exists an appropriate application of robust risk-assessment procedures (e.g. Integrated Financial Risk Assessments). ➢ There is a clear procedure for dealing with unexpected risks, and mechanisms through which auditors can seek advice and recourse. ➢ An appropriate level of risk tolerance is established by entity management and communicated clearly to internal audit as well as to all staff of the entity. • Ensuring financial transactions are adequately identified and recorded (i.e. no "off the books" expenditures or non-identified accounts"). • Monitoring cash payments or payments in kind. • Ensuring that information is kept for sufficient periods and not prematurely destroyed (cfr. OECD, UNODC, World Bank, 2013). • Cross-referencing public expenditure information to detect irregularities within and across sectors.
	Guaranteeing the independence of auditing institution or auditors	• Auditors are subject to specific code of conduct regarding their contacts with the contractors. • Excluding auditing institutions from future public investment audit if they are found in wrongdoings (e.g. receiving bribes, using false information in their reports). • Creating specialised oversight bodies to apply strict procedures for controlling costs and monitoring progress to ensure that projects were built on time and within budget. • There is control of the controllers – e.g. internal audit is overseen by external audit, which is in turn overseen by another objective external body.
	Providing adequate capacity and resources to provide timely and reliable audits	• Ensuring that audit functions are adequately resourced. • Establishing systems and databases on which auditees can draw reliable information about ongoing public works. • Promulgating technical skills to employ innovative technological advancements that ensure more reliable audits and data.

The OECD has developed the following checklist to assist governments and private sector actors in mitigating corruption risks in public investment by identifying corruption entry points over the entire public investment cycle. This instrument can be applied at national, sub-national and local levels, and across sectors, including transport, construction, extractive industries, and energy supply, taking into account the needs and characteristics of the specific investment at stake.

Essential elements applicable to all phases

There are certain measures that should be instituted throughout the policy cycle to mitigate corruption risks. They are not unique to a particular stage or phase, but rather are critical throughout. The following questions and answers may serve as guidance in how to prevent corrupt practices in all phases.

Q1. Are there any measures to prevent public officials and private sector employees from accepting or demanding bribes?

Governments could address these issues through:

- Developing codes of conduct for public officials (see Box 2.1 as an example), who are for instance in charge of tender documents or delivering construction permits, that include:
  - a clear mission of the organisation, as well as its values and principles and the linkages with standards of professional conduct
  - visible guidelines on probity
  - clear definitions on what constitutes a corruption risk
  - guidelines on how public servants deal with the ethical dilemmas, prejudices and grey areas that are encountered in everyday work
  - sanctions for integrity breaches, including administrative, disciplinary and criminal.

Box 2.1. **New Zealand's standards of integrity and conduct**

The current New Zealand Code of Conduct for civil servants came into force on 30 November 2007. The code is delivered as a one-page document, affirming the broad characteristics of public service, which should be fair, impartial, responsible and trustworthy. The code only provides general rules of behaviour, without providing specific advice on how to behave in real-world situations. However, the Code of Conduct is not a self-standing document, as it is provided along with "Understanding the Code of Conduct - Guidance for State Servants"[1], a guide for public employees, which explains the content of the code.

Fair

We must:

- treat everyone fairly and with respect
- be professional and responsive
- work to make government services accessible and effective
- strive to make a difference to the well-being of New Zealand and all its people.

Impartial

We must:

- maintain the political neutrality required to enable us to work with current and future governments

Box 2.1. **New Zealand's standards of integrity and conduct** *(continued)*

- carry out the functions of our organisation, unaffected by our personal beliefs
- support our organisation to provide robust and unbiased advice
- respect the authority of the government of the day.

Responsible

We must:

- act lawfully and objectively
- use our organisation's resources carefully and only for intended purposes
- treat information with care and use it only for proper purposes
- work to improve the performance and efficiency of our organisation.

Trustworthy

We must:

- be honest
- work to the best of our abilities
- ensure our actions are not affected by our personal interests or relationships
- never misuse our position for personal gain
- decline gifts or benefits that place us under any obligation or perceived influence
- avoid any activities, work or non-work, that may harm the reputation of our organisation or of the State Service.

1. Available at www.ssc.govt.nz/code-guidance-stateservants.

Source: New Zealand State Services Commission (2007), "Standards of Integrity and Conduct", www.ssc.govt.nz/sites/all/files/Code-of-conduct-StateServices.pdf.

- Providing training on the organisation's code of conduct and ethical values, as well as standards for public procurement to ensure the wide awareness and understanding of the objectives of the code of conduct, the importance of ethical behaviour and basic principles guiding the procurement process (see Box 2.2).

Box 2.2. UNDP/CIPS co-operation on procurement certification

The United Nations Development Programme (UNDP) offers specialised procurement training and certification to staff from the United Nations (UN) system, non-governmental organisations, international development financing institutions and their borrowers, and governments. UNDP procurement certification courses are accredited by the Chartered Institute of Purchasing and Supply (CIPS) assuring compliance with high international qualification standards as well as offering participants access to a worldwide community of procurement professionals.

All procurement certification course content at Introductory (Level 2), Advanced (Level 3), and Diploma (Level 4) levels is tailored to reflect common United Nations and public procurement rules, policies, practices, and procedures – hereby offering a unique qualification system customised to UN and public procurement requirements. All training courses employ modern adult participatory learning methods. Each training module commences with an overview of the rules, procedures and/or theory of the subject in question, and is then followed by case studies, group discussions or exercises. This creates a forum for participants to apply theory and methods to real cases and to foster productive knowledge sharing.

Source: UNDP (n.d.), "UNDP/CIPS Cooperation on Procurement Training and Certification", www.undp.org/content/undp/en/home/operations/procurement/procurement_training.html (accessed on 20 October 2015).

- Ensuring that the public sector develops and implements codes of conduct for private sector employees (see Boxes 2.3 and 2.4 as examples) that include:
  - clear examples of activities that will compromise the ethical behaviour of the business when working closely with the public sector.
  - punishments for integrity breaches, including administrative, disciplinary and criminal breaches.

Box 2.3. International Federation of Consulting Engineers' Code of Ethics

Responsibility to society and the consulting industry

The consulting engineer shall:

- accept the responsibility of the consulting industry to society
- seek solutions that are compatible with the principles of sustainable development
- at all times uphold the dignity, standing and reputation of the consulting industry.

Competence

The consulting engineer shall:

- maintain knowledge and skills at levels consistent with development in technology, legislation and management, and apply due skill, care and diligence in the services rendered to the client

Box 2.3. **International Federation of Consulting Engineers' Code of Ethics** *(continued)*

- perform services only when competent to perform them.

Integrity

The consulting engineer shall:

- act at all times in the legitimate interest of the client and provide all services with integrity and faithfulness.

Impartiality

The consulting engineer shall:

- be impartial in the provision of professional advice, judgement or decision
- inform the client of any potential conflict of interest that might arise in the performance of services to the client
- not accept remuneration which prejudices independent judgement.

Fairness to others

The consulting engineer shall:

- promote the concept of "Quality-Based Selection" (QBS)
- neither carelessly nor intentionally do anything to injure the reputation or business of others
- neither directly nor indirectly attempt to take the place of another consulting engineer, already appointed for a specific work
- not take over the work of another consulting engineer before notifying the consulting engineer in question, and without being advised in writing by the client of the termination of the prior appointment for that work
- in the event of being asked to review the work of another, behave in accordance with appropriate conduct and courtesy.

Corruption

The consulting engineer shall:

- neither offer nor accept remuneration of any kind which, in perception or in effect, either: *i)* seeks to influence the process of selection or compensation of consulting engineers and/or their clients; or *ii)* seeks to affect the consulting engineer's impartial judgement
- co-operate fully with any legitimately constituted investigative body which makes inquiry into the administration of any contract for services or construction.

Source: Adapted from International Federation of Consulting Engineers (FIDIC)'s Code of Ethics, http://fidic.org/about-fidic/fidic-policies/fidic-code-ethics (accessed on 20 October 2015).

Box 2.4. Code of Practice for the South Australian Construction Industry

The Code of Practice for the South Australian Construction Industry and its Implementation Guidelines is a statement of the principles that the industry wants to apply to a range of procedures from project conception and initiation, through tendering and construction, to project completion. The Code of Practice for the South Australian Construction Industry and its Implementation Guidelines aims to: *i)* establish standards of behaviour and standards for the management of relationships between parties in various roles within the industry; and *ii)* introduce reforms as agreed by the industry and by the Government of South Australia. The Code of Practice for the South Australian Construction Industry and its Implementation Guidelines are mandatory on all South Australian Government funded and managed construction projects.

The code was initiated by the private sector of the State's construction industry as part of the ongoing process of industry development. It is a tool to assist the industry to be nationally competitive by strengthening the best practices that already exist and by introducing new best practices. The code supports the introduction of asset management policies by the Government of South Australia and the achievement of these delivery standards by the private sector.

The main objectives of the code are the following: *i)* promote action to improve efficiency and productivity; *ii)* eliminate unacceptable practices including those that result from short-term and expedient decision making; *iii)* establish standards which the industry requires to be observed; *iv)* improve performance and maintain good practice of all participants in the South Australian Construction Industry; *v)* promote the highest standards within the construction industry by seeking the commitment of all those covered by this code to comply with the full spirit and intent of all laws, regulations and standards applying to the industry; *vi)* obtain the best value by sharing risks equitably through assigning each risk to the party most able to bear the risk; *vii)* promote the application of sensible and proper practices for the long-term benefit of the industry and all parties involved; *viii)* seek to secure improvements in practice that have been achieved so far, *ix)* seek to promote goodwill in the industry and prevent disputes by observing agreements, statutory requirements and obligations of employment.

Source: Government of South Australia (2013), "Code of Practice for the South Australian Construction Industry", Department of Planning, Transport and Infrastructure, www.infrastructure.sa.gov.au/BuildingManagement/policies.

- Applying strong legal sanctions to the contractors who offer bribe payments, such as restrictions on participation in future investment projects or other public procurement processes (see Boxes 2.5 and 2.6).

Box 2.5. Agreement for Mutual Enforcement of Debarment Decisions: Cross-debarment

The African Development Bank Group, the Asian Development Bank, the European Bank for Reconstruction and Development, the Inter-American Development Bank Group and the World Bank Group signed the Agreement for Mutual Enforcement of Debarment Decisions in April, 2010. The participating institutions enforce debarment decisions made by another participating institution with respect to the agreed four sanctionable practices, including: *i)* fraudulent practice; *ii)* corrupt practice; *iii)* coercive practice, and *iv)* collusive practice.

Source: CoST (Construction Sector Transparency Initiative) (2013), "Establishing a multi-stakeholder group and national secretariat", www.constructiontransparency.org/documentdownload.axd? documentresourceid=29.

Box 2.6. Debarment in Canada

The Public Works and Government Services Canada (PWGSC) Integrity Framework establishes that a supplier is ineligible to do business with PWGSC for ten years following a conviction or a guilty plea with a conditional or absolute discharge for any of the following Canadian or similar foreign offences:

- fraud against the government under the Criminal Code of Canada
- fraud under the Financial Administration Act
- payment of a contingency fee to a person to whom the Lobbying Act applies
- corruption, collusion, bid-rigging or any other anti-competitive activity under the Competition Act
- money laundering
- participation in activities of criminal organisations
- income and excise tax evasion
- bribing a foreign public official
- offences in relation to drug trafficking
- extortion
- bribery of judicial officers
- bribery of officers
- secret commissions
- criminal breach of contracts
- fraudulent manipulation of stock exchange transactions
- prohibited insider trading
- forgery and other offences resembling forgery
- falsification of books and documents.

In order for bids to be admissible following the ten-year debarment period, a record suspension must be obtained, or capacities restored by the Governor in Council, for fraud-related offences under the Criminal Code of Canada or the Financial Administration Act.

Source: Public Works and Government Services Canada (2015), "Government of Canada's Integrity Regime", www.tpsgc-pwgsc.gc.ca/ci-if/ci-if-eng.html.

Q2. Are there measures in place to adequately identify and manage potential and apparent conflict-of-interest situations?

Governments could address this issue through:

- Identifying and mitigating conflict-of-interest situations through legislation, codes of conduct or guidelines (see Box 2.7 as an example).

Box 2.7. **Principles and code of conduct for procurement in Spain**

With the aim of contributing to excellence in administrative activities within the area of procurement, the Office for Supervision and Evaluation of Public Procurement has compiled in this code the basic principles and good practice that have already been integrated into the day-to-day activities of the Ministries of the Administration of the *Generalitat* of Catalonia and the entities that form part of its public sector. New content for establishing the code of conduct and recommendations is also contained, contributed by the Working Group for the Promotion and Improvement of Procurement Processes, constituted within the Consultative Board on Administrative Procurement of the *Generalitat* of Catalonia, the Anti-Fraud Office of Catalonia, the Catalan Competition Authority, the Association of Secretaries, Mediators and Treasurers of the Catalan Local Administration, as well as business and trade union organisations.

The aim of the code is to consolidate the Code of Ethics in Procurement as part of the culture and values of procurement bodies. The good procurement practice included in the code is structured in the following sections:

1. the specifying of the basic principles and ethical values that must govern the procurement process
2. the identification of specific conduct of interest with a view to drawing up the guidelines to follow in a variety of possible real, specific circumstances
3. the specifying of especially interesting contractual practices
4. the raising of awareness, training and the monitoring of the ethical commitment.

With the creation of the Ethics Committee in Procurement of the *Generalitat* of Catalonia, made up of representatives from the ministries and entities of the *Generalitat* of Catalonia and belonging to the Presidency Department, a follow up and a continuous updating of the code in the Administration of the *Generalitat* and the entities of its public sector will be carried out.

Source: Codi de principis i conductes recomanables en la contractació pública (Principles and Code of Conduct for Procurement), http://transparencia.gencat.cat/ca/Contractacio/criteris-interpretatius-acords-i-directrius/codi-de-principis-i-conductes-recomanables-en-la-contractacio-publica/

- Providing clear examples and situations of private interests that may lead to potential conflict-of-interest situations in legislation, codes of conduct and/or guidelines, including on gifts, hospitality, previous employment, outside positions, assets and liabilities.
- Setting specific restrictions and prohibitions on public officials (especially in decision-making positions) working in the public procurement authority or responsible for public procurement in government bodies (see Box 2.8).

Box 2.8. **Turkey's 2002 Public Procurement Law**

With the 2002 Public Procurement Law (PPL), the Public Procurement Authority (PPA) was established as an administratively and financially autonomous entity at the central governmental level to regulate and monitor public procurement. In order to prevent problems encountered previously, measures were introduced by the law to prevent pressures from interest groups and set higher ethical standards for officials, in particular:

- Members of the Public Procurement Board are appointed by the Council of Ministers and must fulfil criteria, including higher education, more than 12 years of experience in public institutions, and knowledge and experience in the field of national and international public procurement procedures. Candidates shall have no past or present relationship of membership or task with any political party. Members of the Board are nominated for a five-year term and once appointed, cannot be revoked before the expiry of their term.
- Members of the Board, except for some legally defined exceptions, cannot be involved in any official or private jobs, trade or freelance activities, and cannot be a shareholder or manager in any kind of partnerships based on commercial purposes.

Source: OECD (2007), *Integrity in Public Procurement: Good Practice From A to Z*, www.oecd.org/development/effectiveness/38588964.pdf, pp. 79-80.

- Providing public officials in "at risk" areas with specific codes of conduct, especially for those who have higher interaction with the private sector (see Box 2.9).

Box 2.9. **Canada's Code of Conduct for Procurement**

The Code of Conduct for Procurement provides all those involved in the procurement process – public servants and vendors alike – with a clear statement of mutual expectations to ensure a common basic understanding among all participants in accountable, ethical and transparent procurement. The Code of Conduct for Procurement applies to all transactions entered into by Public Works and Government Services of Canada (PWGSC) either for their own procurements or on behalf of a client department.

The Code of Conduct for Procurement gives guidance regarding:

- responsibilities of public servants
- conflict-of-interest measures
- post-employment measures
- vendors' responsibility regarding solicitation and contract provisions
- vendors' duty to respect the responsibilities of public servants
- vendor complaints and procedural safeguards
- sanctions.

Source: Public Works and Government Services Canada (2014), "Context and purpose of the Code", www.tpsgc-pwgsc.gc.ca/app-acq/cndt-cndct/contexte-context-eng.html.

- Requiring public officials to disclose their family members' private interests where potential conflicts of interest may arise (see Boxes 2.10 and 2.11).

Box 2.10. **Conflict-of-interest management during tender evaluation in Australia**

The Government of South Australia's Department of Planning, Transport and Infrastructure (DPTI) addresses ways to address potential and material conflict-of-interest situations during the procurement process through the Procurement Management Framework. It states that the DPTI staff member should notify the evaluation panel chairperson as soon as he/she notices any apparent conflict-of-interest situation. Even though a potential conflict of interest will not necessarily preclude a person from being involved in the evaluation process, it is declared and can be independently assessed.

It also lists situations that would be considered as a material conflict of interest of a staff in relation to a company submitting a tender, including: *i)* a significant shareholding in a small private company that is submitting a tender; *ii)* having an immediate relative (e.g. son, daughter, partner, sibling) employed by a company which is tendering, even though that person is not involved in the preparation of the tender and winning the tender would have a material impact on the company; *iii)* having a relative who is involved in the preparation of the tender to be submitted by a company; *iv)* exhibiting a bias or partiality for or against a tender (e.g. because of events that occurred during a previous contract); *v)* a person, engaged under a contract to assist DPTI with the assessment, assessing a direct competitor who is submitting a tender; *vi)* regularly socialising with an employee of tenderer who is involved with the preparation of the tender; *vii)* having received gifts, hospitality or similar benefits from a tenderer in the period leading up to the call of tenders; *viii)* having recently left the employment of a tenderer; or *ix)* considering an offer of future employment or some other inducement from a tenderer.

Source: Government of South Australia (n.d.), "DPTI Procurement Practices and Policies", www.dpti.sa.gov.au/open_government/proactive_disclosure/details_of_procurement_practices_within_departments.

Box 2.11. **Conflict-of-interest management in infrastructure projects in the Philippines**

The Bidding Document provided by the Department of Transportation and Communication of the Philippines for the Bicol International Airport Development Project states that bidders with conflicting interests shall be disqualified from participating in the procurement process. The document lists detailed cases of bidders with conflicting interest situations, examples of which include: a bidder having controlling shareholders in common with another bidder; a bidder receiving or having received any direct or indirect subsidy from any other bidder; or a bidder who participated as a consultant in the preparation of the design or technical specifications of the goods and related services that are the subject of the bid.

Furthermore, in accordance with the Implementing Rules and Regulations of Republic Act No. 9183 ("Government Procurement Reform Act"), all bidding documents shall be accompanied by a sworn affidavit of the bidder that he/she is not related to the Head of the Procuring Entity, members of the Bid and Awards Committee (BAC), a member of the Technical Working Group (TWG), members of the BAC Secretariat, the head of the Project Management Office (PMO) or the end-user unit, and the project consultants, by consanguinity or affinity up to the third civil degree.

Source: Government of the Republic of the Philippines (2014), "Procurement of Infrastructure Projects: BICOL International Airport Development Project", www.dotc.gov.ph/images/Public_Bidding/CivilWorks/_Air_Sector/2014/NewLegazpiApt--BIADP_P2a/BidDocs_BIADP_Pkg2A_Clean_WithEdits_SGD.pdf.

Q3. Are there measures in place to regulate and limit the use of confidential information by public officials?

Governments could address this issue through:

- Cancelling retrospectively the decisions based on confidential information.
- Setting up mechanisms that prevent confidential information, authority or influence from being used for personal gain or for improper advantage of other businesses and non-profit organisations.

Q4. Are there mechanisms in place for the government and the private sector to provide protection for employees to report wrongdoings or breaches of integrity?

Governments and business could address this issue through:

- Providing consistent advice and support to staff in case of questions or having witnessed misconduct and integrity breaches, such as through a whistleblower hotline, and providing effective whistleblower protections for those who report misconduct in good faith (see Box 2.12 as an example).

Box 2.12. **Whistleblower hotline in Austria**

In March 2013, the Ministry of Justice set up a whistleblower hotline on the homepage of the Public Prosecutor's Office against Corruption and White Collar Crime. As of September 2013, approximately 590 notifications were sent to the platform. Only 53 of those notifications were not relevant. The whistleblower hotline has a test phase of two years.

The Federal Ministry of Justice's whistleblowing website enables investigators from the Public Prosecutor's Office against Corruption and White Collar Crime (*Zentrale Staatsanwaltschaft zur Verfolgung von Wirtschaftsstrafsachen und Korruption*; *WKStA*) to get in direct contact with whistleblowers, with the anonymity of the latter being assured. In that event, the whistleblower is entitled to decide whether he/she would like to remain anonymous or to identify him- or herself to the investigators.

Sources: Transparency International (2013), "Whistleblowing in Europe", www.transparency.de/fileadmin/pdfs/Themen/Hinweisgebersysteme/EU_Whistleblower_Report_final_web.pdf, p. 25; Shoneherr (2013a), "Austria: Whistleblower hotline is launched online", www.schoenherr.eu/knowledge/knowledge-detail/austria-whistleblower-hotline-is-launched-online/.

- Developing guidelines to report wrongdoing in case of integrity breaches or mismanagement and providing effective protections for those who report such wrongdoing in good faith.
- Providing effective protection ensuring that private and public sector employees, as well as their careers, are protected, in case they report wrongdoing in good faith (see Box 2.13).

Box 2.13. **Comprehensive protection of public interest whistleblowers in Korea**

Korea's Act on the Protection of Public Interest Whistleblowers provides protection to whistleblowers who report any violation of public interest in both the public and private sector. Whistleblowers are protected from:

a. removal from office, release from office, dismissal or any other unfavourable personnel action equivalent to the loss of status at work

b. disciplinary action, suspension from office, reduction in pay, demotion, restriction on promotion and any other unfair personnel actions

c. work reassignment, transfer, denial of duties, rearrangement of duties or any other personnel actions that are against the whistleblower's will

d. discrimination in the performance evaluation, peer review, etc. and subsequent discrimination in the payment of wages, bonuses, etc.

e. the cancellation of education, training or other self-development opportunities, the restriction or removal of budget, work force or other available resources, the suspension of access to security information or classified information; the cancellation of authorisation to handle security information or classified information; or any other discrimination or measure detrimental to the working conditions of the whistleblower;

f. putting the whistleblower's name on a blacklist as well as the release of such a blacklist, bullying, the use of violence and abusive language toward the whistleblower, or any other action that causes psychological or physical harm to the whistleblower;

g. unfair audit or inspection of the whistleblower's work as well as the disclosure of the results of such an audit or inspection

h. the cancellation of a license or permit, or any other action that causes administrative disadvantages to the whistleblower.

Source: Korea's Act on the Protection of Public Interest Whistleblowers, Act No. 10472, Mar. 29, 2011, Article 2 (6).

Q5. Are there measures in place in the private sector to ensure support and commitment from senior management in the prevention of corruption in public investment?

Business could address this issue through:

- Demonstrating visible and active commitment by the Board of Directors or equivalent body to the implementation of the enterprise's programme.
- Demonstrating strong, explicit and visible support and commitment from senior management to the company's internal controls, ethics and compliance programmes or measures for preventing and detecting foreign bribery (see Box 2.14).

Box 2.14. **British Petroleum's and Vodafone's anti-corruption statements**

British Petroleum

"We operate in some of the world's highest risk countries from an anti-bribery and corruption perspective, as measured by Transparency International's Corruption Perceptions Index. We have a responsibility to our shareholders and to the countries and communities in which we do business to be ethical and lawful in all our dealings. Our code of conduct explicitly states that we do not tolerate bribery and corruption in any of its forms. Our group-wide anti-bribery and corruption policy applies to all BP-operated businesses. The policy governs areas such as appropriate clauses in contracts, risk assessments and training. We target training on a risk basis and to those employees for whom it is thought to be most relevant, for example, given specific incidents or the nature or location of their role."

Vodafone

"To uphold our business principles, Vodafone and our suppliers and our business partners are expected to have a zero-tolerance policy in relation to bribery and corruption. A comprehensive compliance programme supports the awareness and implementation of this policy across our global business. A key part of Vodafone's anti-bribery programme involves communicating with our suppliers and our business partners to ensure that they have adopted a similar zero tolerance approach to bribery which they are supporting through a compliance programme involving appropriate tone from the top, policy, training and awareness raising, due diligence, whistle-blowing procedures and monitoring. This is reflected within our Code of Ethical Purchasing V2.0. Vodafone Supply Chain have a significant role to play in the in the decision-making process to choose suppliers and the giving or accepting of gifts, corporate hospitality or entertainment can risk leaving Vodafone and its suppliers open to misinterpretation when it comes to ensuring the honesty and transparency of this decision-making process. Suppliers are requested to be aware and respect that Vodafone Supply Chain operates a 'No Gift' policy and any inappropriate hospitality will be refused. Please be reminded that Vodafone's 'Speak Up' programme for suppliers provides an anonymous and confidential whistle-blowing mechanism for anyone to raise an incident of unethical behaviour for further investigation."

Sources: BP (British Petroleum) (n.d.), "Our code of conduct", www.bp.com/en/global/corporate/sustainability/how-we-operate/our-code-of-conduct.html; Vodafone (n.d.), "Anti-bribery", http://vodafone360.com/content/index/about/about_us/suppliers/anti_bribery.html .

- Adopting anti-corruption codes of conduct for businesses (see Box 2.15).

Box 2.15. **APEC Anti-corruption Code of Conduct for Business**

Asia-Pacific Economic Cooperation (APEC) leaders have acknowledged the importance of curbing corruption in business and promoting business integrity and transparency in the private sector, and have thus developed the APEC Anti-corruption Code of Conduct for Business. The code specifically lists the following elements:

1. Prohibition of bribery; that all forms of bribes shall be prohibited.
2. Programme to Counter Bribery; that the enterprises, in consultation with their employees, should develop a programme reflecting the characteristics and specificities of the business which should apply to all controlled subsidiaries, foreign and domestic.

Box 2.15. **APEC Anti-corruption Code of Conduct for Business** *(continued)*

3. Provision of clear scope and guidelines with regard to charitable contributions, gifts, hospitality, expenses, facilitation payments and political contributions.

4. Implementation of the programme via communication, management leadership especially that of the Board and the CEO, appropriate financial recording and auditing mechanisms, human resources management reflecting the enterprise's commitment to it, raising awareness, monitoring and review, training, etc.

Source: APEC (n.d.), "Anti-corruption Code of Conduct for Business", www.apec.org/Groups/SOM-Steering-Committee-on-Economic-and-Technical-Cooperation/Task-Groups/~/media/Files/Groups/ACT/07_act_codebrochure.ashx (accessed on 20 October 2015).

Q6. Are there measures in place for governments and companies to promote and incentivise integrity and compliance together?

Governments and business could address this issue together through:

- Taking a holistic approach to promoting business integrity, especially in the area of public investment, given that these transactions are especially prone to the risk of corruption and other types of misconduct (i.e. fraud, bid-rigging, money-laundering, conflicts of interest, etc.) The OECD is considering this type of approach to promoting business integrity with the new OECD Trust and Business Project (www.oecd.org/daf/ca/trust-business.htm). This approach could include assessing the following measures for creating a culture of integrity in companies doing business with governments, many of which are included in the OECD's *Good Practice Guidance on Internal Controls, Ethics and Compliance*:
  - reflecting the company's commitment in the fight against corruption in recruitment, promotion, training and performance evaluation.
  - ensuring that employees will not suffer retaliation, discriminatory or disciplinary action for refusing to pay bribes, even if such refusal may result in the company losing business
  - providing regular trainings to employees on integrity and anti-corruption measures
  - implementing special policies for particular risk areas such as facilitation payments; conflict of interest; solicitation and extortion; and special types of expenditures, such as gifts, hospitality, travel and entertainment, political contributions, and charitable contributions and sponsorships.
- Multi-stakeholder initiatives, or collective actions, are an efficient way to promote transparency and accountability in publicly financed construction (see Box 2.16).

Box 2.16. **The Construction Sector Transparency Initiative (CoST)**

CoST works with government, industry and civil society to promote the disclosure of information on public investment in infrastructure. The information includes 38 data points – the "Infrastructure Data Standard" – that are routinely and periodically disclosed over the whole project lifecycle. The information is designed to inform and empower stakeholders and enable them to hold decision makers to account.

Public procuring entities are responsible for disclosing information in a form that is accessible to stakeholders. An independent Assurance Team reviews the disclosed information and produces a concise report that speaks to the veracity of the information and identifies any gaps or causes for concern.

CoST is now active in 14 countries – Afghanistan, El Salvador, Ethiopia, Honduras, Guatemala, Malawi, Philippines, Tanzania, Thailand, Uganda, Ukraine, United Kingdom, Vietnam and Zambia. Each programme is overseen by a multi-stakeholder group (MSG) comprising representatives from government, industry and civil society. A new programme might start on a "voluntary" basis where there is no legal requirement to disclose information, but eventually information disclosure is institutionalised through the establishment of a "Formal Disclosure Requirement".

Improvements in transparency and accountability help to create a business environment in which corruption is less likely to occur and helps drive improvements in management and efficiency. Ultimately, improvements in transparency and accountability contribute to better value for money and better quality infrastructure and services.

Source: Adapted from www.constructiontransparency.org (accessed on 20 October 2015).

1. Needs definition and selection phase

The identification and selection process of investment projects could involve significant discretion on the part of public officials, along with the participation of multiple stakeholders, which makes this stage prone to corruption. Specific regulations for each stakeholder should be clearly stated and communicated, and potential conflict-of-interest situations should be adequately identified and managed for the public officials involved in the process.

Enhancing transparency and public participation can contribute to ensuring that the process is carried out based on genuine policy priorities. In addition, addressing the treatment of confidential information and depoliticising the problem identification and public investment selection could greatly help to limit undue influence in the process. The following questions and answers may offer a guide to preventing corrupt practices in this phase.

Q7. Are there measures in place to ensure that public investment decisions are based on national, regional or sectorial objectives?

Governments could address this issue through:

- Providing online platforms where the public is invited to inform national infrastructure priorities.

- Setting up an independent body responsible for assessing the national infrastructure needs.
- Co-ordinating with sub-national governments to ensure that strategic priorities for investment are well aligned across levels of government (OECD, 2014a) (see Box 2.17).

Box 2.17. **Infrastructure Australia and the national/sub-national platform of dialogue**

Infrastructure Australia

The central government created an advisory body, Infrastructure Australia (IA), to co-ordinate with the states for investments of national importance. The body was established in 2008 to advise the central government on investment priorities in the transport, communication, water and energy sectors and to help states identify infrastructure projects that are a national priority. IA assesses the states' applications for funding under the Building Australia Fund (BAF), the Commonwealth's main mechanism to finance critical infrastructure projects.

National/sub-national platform of dialogue

The Council of Australian Governments (COAG) is the main forum for the development and implementation of inter-jurisdictional policy. It is composed of the Australian Prime Minister as its chair, State Premiers, Territory Chief Ministers and the President of the Australian Local Government Association. Through COAG, the federal and sub-national governments have endorsed national guidelines on public-private partnerships, agreed to a national port strategy, and concluded intergovernmental agreements on heavy vehicles, rail and maritime safety. COAG also receives regular reports from Infrastructure Australia.

Source: OECD (2014b), "Toolkit on effective public investment across levels of government – Australia", www.oecd.org/effective-public-investment-toolkit/australia.pdf.

Q8. Are there measures in place to prevent the selection of public investment from favouring a particular interest group/individual over the public interest?

Governments could address this issue through:

- Rendering the decision-making process more transparent by:
  - making relevant information publicly available through channels such as websites and newsletters (see Box 2.18)
  - ensuring that this information reaches civil society and the media, who play a particular role in keeping stakeholders accountable

Box 2.18. **The United Kingdom's National Infrastructure Planning website**

The Planning Act 2008 process was introduced to streamline the decision-making process for nationally significant infrastructure projects, making it fairer and faster for communities and developers alike. The Planning Inspectorate, the government agency responsible for examining planning applications for nationally significant infrastructure projects, has developed a website to allow citizens to find out about proposed major infrastructure projects within England and Wales.

The projects listed are those:

- where the developer has advised the Planning Inspectorate in writing that he/she intends to submit an application in the future
- where an application has already been made to the Planning Inspectorate and is undergoing the development consent process
- where a proposal has been decided.

Withdrawn projects are displayed for a period of time before they are removed from the website.

Source: UK Planning Inspectorate, National Infrastructure Planning website, http://infrastructure.planningportal.gov.uk/ (accessed on 20 October 2015).

  - publishing information and reports regarding long-term national and development plans
  - increasing citizen participation through participatory budgets (see Box 2.19).

Box 2.19. **Participatory budgeting, Porto Alegre, Brazil**

Participatory budgeting (PB) began more than a decade ago in Porto Alegre, the Capital of the State of *Rio Grande do Sul*, one of the most populated cities in South Brazil.

Participatory budgeting is a process through which citizens present their demands and priorities for civic improvement, and influence the budget allocations made by their municipalities through discussions and negotiations.

Since 1989, budget allocations for public welfare works in Porto Alegre have been made only after the recommendations of public delegates and approval by the city council. Participatory budgeting has resulted in improved facilities for the people of Porto Alegre.

The Participative Budget has proved that the democratic and transparent administration of resources is the only way to avoid corruption and mishandling of public funds. Despite certain technocratic opinions, the popular participation has provided efficient spending, effective where it has to be and with results in public works and actions of great importance for the population. Since its beginning, the projects decided by the Participative Budget represent investments over USD 700 million, mainly in urban infrastructure and in upgrading the quality level of the population.

Sources: Adapted from World Bank (2015), "Participatory budgeting in Brazil", *Empowerment Case Studies*, http://siteresources.worldbank.org/INTEMPOWERMENT/Resources/14657_Partic-Budg-Brazil-web.pdf; UNESCO (2015), "The experience of the participative budget in Porto Alegre, Brazil", www.unesco.org/most/southa13.htm.

- Increasing citizen participation through a website for citizens to prioritise public investments (see Boxes 2.20 and 2.21).

Box 2.20. **Transparent Chennai in India**

Transparent Chennai is an Indian website that aggregates, creates and disseminates data and research about important civic issues facing the city of Chennai, including those issues facing the poor. The organisation aims to empower residents by providing them useful, easy-to-understand information that can better highlight citizen needs, shed light on government performance, and improve their lives in the city. The goal is to enable residents, especially the poor, to have a greater voice in planning and city governance. The organisation's work is unique because it actually creates maps and data to understand issues facing city residents. They believe that a lack of data has sometimes allowed government to evade its responsibilities to provide basic entitlements to all city residents, and to exercise force with impunity over informal settlements and workers. They work closely with individuals and citizens' groups to create data that can help them counter inaccurate or incomplete government data, and make better claims on the government for their rights and entitlements.

Some of the data is available in the form of interactive maps, which can be layered on top of one another to contextualise information. Mapping can provide useful information to citizens, identify gaps in government data, create insights into policy making, help create more accountability for elected representatives and bureaucracies, and help residents to "think spatially" at a time of rapid urbanisation.

Team members also conduct in-depth research into selected issues of importance in the city, including urban governance, electoral accountability, participatory planning processes, pedestrian issues, slums, sanitation, and solid waste management, details about all of which can be found on the site. They regularly disseminate their data and research through the organisation's website, blog, mailing list, publications, meetings with citizens, researchers, and policymakers, in conferences, and through the media, in both English and in Tamil.

Source: www.transparentchennai.com/about/ (accessed on 20 October 2015).

Box 2.21. **Rethinking public participation in infrastructure projects**

Pointing to the fact that the mission of any public infrastructure and construction (PIC) project is to improve the well-being of society, the University of Hong Kong launched a research project on innovative ideas to promote public participation in infrastructure projects.

As some of these projects might impact the environment and affect the habitat of local residents, it is not unusual to attract criticism or even opposition from various stakeholder groups. Consequently, there is an increasing concern about the effectiveness of public participation in PIC projects.

The authors strive to examine the salient elements of public participation by considering the questions of "who", "what" and "how" in the process. The research project paper begins by reviewing the international public participation practices and the models proposed by various researchers. The key aspects to be considered during the public participation process are then highlighted. The paper concludes by proposing a comprehensive participatory framework for PIC projects, especially those of a highly sensitive nature. The results show that the viewpoints

Box 2.21. **Rethinking public participation in infrastructure projects** *(continued)*

of various stakeholders can be rather diverse, and it is necessary to ensure that a consensus is reached at different project stages through a well-planned, whole-cycle participatory exercise in order to maximise the chance of project success. More importantly, better acceptance towards other views and more education on the importance of public participation are needed to ensure that society benefits from economic and social development without sacrificing the rights and best interests of minority groups.

Source: University of Hong Kong (2012), "Rethinking public participation in infrastructure projects", http://hub.hku.hk/bitstream/10722/159430/1/content.pdf?accept=1.

- Inviting relevant groups to participate in the decision-making process:
  - finding the right mix of participants and ensuring that no group is inadvertently excluded
  - carrying out stakeholder mapping and analysis (see Box 2.22).

Box 2.22. **Public inquiry in the construction of Heathrow's Terminal 5, United Kingdom**

The construction of Heathrow Airport Terminal 5 (T5) was the largest construction project in Europe in the early 2000s.

The construction of Heathrow's Terminal 5 also holds the record of the longest public inquiry in the history of the United Kingdom, which lasted nearly four years. The public inquiry cost GBP 80 million, heard 700 witnesses and generated 100 000 pages of transcripts. The Secretary of State gave his approval to the project after reviewing the public inquiry report, and a number of conditions and limitations were imposed to take into account the complaints of local communities regarding noise and pollution.

The British Airports Authority (BAA) claimed that the terminal was needed to cope with the projected rise in numbers of passengers from around 58 million at the time to 80 million in 2013, to maintain Heathrow's position as a world airport hub. BAA argued that because aircraft were getting larger, the number of flights would only increase by 8%. BAA told the public inquiry that it was prepared to accept a cap on aircraft noise at 1994 levels and a limit on the number of night flights at then current levels. It maintained that noise would not increase because engines were getting quieter and noise monitoring was improving. BAA said that if Terminal 5 was rejected, the South East of England would run out of airport capacity in five years, with damaging effects on the economy. BAA also claimed that opinion polls showed a growing number of local residents supported the terminal.

The London Chamber of Commerce launched a campaign, Business for T5, to promote the benefits of expanding the airport. It claimed that overseas visitors would spend an estimated 10 million fewer nights in Britain if Terminal 5 did not go ahead, with a loss of about GBP 1 billion to the hotels sector and another GBP 500 million to the wider tourist industry.

Heathrow has since launched property and noise consultations to develop compensation packages and seek views on how that compensation fund should be used. GBP 550 million was allocated for the noise insulation and property compensation programme.

Source: Butcher, Louise (2014), "Aviation; London Heathrow Airport", *Commons Briefing Papers,* SN01136, http://researchbriefings.parliament.uk/ResearchBriefing/Summary/SN01136. Contains parliamentary information licensed under the Open Parliament Licence v3.0, www.parliament.uk/site-information/copyright/open-parliament-licence/.

- Consulting experts and "outsiders" from the public administration to evaluate the pertinence of the public investment, and publicly disclosing the results of that consultation.
- Securing transparency and integrity in lobbying (OECD Principles on Lobbying):
  - introducing a lobbying registry (see Box 2.23)

Box 2.23. **The EU Transparency Register**

The EU Transparency Register was set up in 2011 to answer core questions such as what interests are being pursued, by whom and with what budgets. The system is operated jointly by the European Parliament and the European Commission.

The new register replaces the one set up by the Commission in 2008, and already contains more than 4 000 organisations. The EU Transparency Register extends its coverage well beyond traditional lobbyists to include law firms, non-governmental organisations (NGOs), think tanks - indeed any organisation or self-employed individual engaged in influencing EU policy making and implementation. This is a step towards the EU's goal of a more participatory democracy.

Registrants have to provide more information than before, such as the number of staff involved in advocacy, the main legislative proposals they have covered, as well as the amount of EU funding they received.

By signing up to the Transparency Register, organisations commit to a Common Code of Conduct pledging, for example, always to identify themselves by name and the entity they work for, and not to obtain information dishonestly. A complaint mechanism and measures to be applied are also outlined for those who break the Code of Conduct.

Source: European Commission (n.d.), "Transparency Register", http://ec.europa.eu/transparencyregister/public/homePage.do?redir=false&locale=en.

- Implementing regulations of revolving doors (e.g. cooling-off period) (see Box 2.24).

Box 2.24. **Revolving doors: Australia and Chile**

Article 7 of Australia's Lobbying Code of Conduct sets a cooling-off period of 18 months for ministers and parliamentary secretaries, and 12 months for ministerial staff. During those periods, the former are prohibited from engaging in lobbying activities pertaining to any matter on which they worked in the last 18 months of employment, and the latter in the last 12 months.

For a period of six months after they leave office, Chile prohibits officials from the executive branch of government from working in or for companies that were under the supervision and control of the public body in which they were previously employed.

Source: OECD (2014c), *Lobbyists, Governments and Public Trust, Volume 3: Implementing the OECD Principles for Transparency and Integrity in Lobbying*, OECD Publishing, Paris, http://dx.doi.org/10.1787/9789264214224-en.

- Ensuring transparency and balanced composition in the advisory group; clear selection, membership and appointment procedures; clear mandate (see Box 2.25).

Box 2.25. EU Register of Commission Expert Groups and Similar Entities

The European Commission created a Register of Commission Expert Groups and Similar Entities in December 2010. It contains information on the types of entities listed, groups' membership, the department running the groups, the procedures used to select members, groups' missions and activities. Stakeholders can thus scrutinise the work of advisory groups which, in turn, could make it less likely that the interests of the few influence outcomes at the expense of the public interest.

Source: OECD (2014c), *Lobbyists, Governments and Public Trust, Volume 3: Implementing the OECD Principles for Transparency and Integrity in Lobbying*, OECD Publishing, Paris, http://dx.doi.org/10.1787/9789264214224-en.

Q9. Are there measures in place to prevent elected public officials from choosing a specific public investment to benefit contractors who contributed to their political campaigns?

Governments could address this issue through:

- Banning certain types of private contributions, in particular:
  - corporations with government contracts or partial government ownership
  - corporate donations, trade unions, etc.
  - foreign corporate donations
  - introducing a limit for private funding.
- Requiring disclosures of information regarding political funding and ensuring that:
  - information is timely, reliable, accessible and intelligible; public disclosure of reports
  - information is complete and includes private donations (see Box 2.26)

Box 2.26. Oversight/information disclosure in the United Kingdom and Italy

In the United Kingdom all parties' reported financial information, i.e. donation/loan reports, campaign expenditure returns and statement of accounts are made available on the Electoral Commission's website. This includes pdf copies of invoices and receipts for campaign expenditure.

In Italy, party financial accounts must be published on the websites of the political parties, the website of the Chamber of Deputies, as well as in newspapers, and the Official Gazette of the State.

Source: OECD (2016), *Financing Democracy: Funding of Political Parties and Election Campaigns and the Risk of Policy Capture,* OECD Public Governance Reviews, OECD Publishing, Paris, http://dx.doi.org/10.1787/ 9789264249455-en.

- Promoting media and civil society scrutiny.
- Ensuring that companies/contractors publish their contributions to political campaigns and political parties online.
- Ensuring independent and efficient oversight by:
  - strengthening the independence of a monitoring body and processes
  - providing capacity through sufficient resources and specialised auditing capacities and methodologies
  - providing for dissuasive and enforceable sanctions in case of breaches (see Box 2.27).

Box 2.27. **Sanctions on non-submission of financial reports in New Zealand**

In New Zealand, non-submission of financial reports can lead to fines. If anonymous donations exceed NZD 1 500 (USD 1 000), the exceeding amount must be paid to the Electoral Management Body. Persons convicted of corrupt practices lose their right to vote for three years, and face imprisonment not exceeding two years. In cases of corrupt or illegal campaign practices, the election of a candidate can be voided.

Source: OECD (2016), *Financing Democracy: Funding of Political Parties and Election Campaigns and the Risk of Policy Capture,* OECD Public Governance Reviews, OECD Publishing, Paris, http://dx.doi.org/10.1787/9789264249455-en.

2. Appraisal phase

It can be difficult to assess the cost of government-led investment projects, and especially infrastructure projects, where comparable information is not often available due to the size of the projects or the scarcity of comparable projects. Due to this, financial, economic, environmental and social feasibility studies have more room for manipulation. It is thus suggested by some experts to use reference class forecasting as an aid in making more accurate estimations of costs and benefits (Flyvbjerg, Garbuio and Lovallo, 2009).

Moreover, guaranteeing the independence of the experts and consultants carrying out the studies may also assist in mitigating corruption risks in this phase. Similarly, a professional and independent audit function can be an important method of deterring and detecting corruption. An *ex ante* audit during the project appraisal should work to deter potential avenues for corruption, requiring risks to be addressed before advancement. However, *ex ante* audits should not be relied upon as the sole check-and-balance, but should be considered one verification method meant to coincide with appropriate due diligence and the application of measured controls. The following questions and answers may serve as guidance in how to prevent corrupt practices in this phase.

Q10. Are there measures in place to ensure that awarding the contract to banks to finance the investment is based on cost and their capacity to finance, and that it is not inflicted by other undue influence?

Governments could address this issue through:

- Ensuring that bankers follow codes of conduct with specific regulations, requiring more scrutiny for those having higher interaction with the public sector (see Box 2.28).

Box 2.28. **Business Conduct Guidelines of *Commerzbank AG* in Germany**

The Business Conduct Guidelines of *Commerzbank AG* address the professional ethics and behaviour of their employees, *inter alia*, by requiring compliance with applicable laws as well as impartiality and the prohibition of accepting or providing gifts. The guidelines also include sections on conflicts of interest, bribery, corruption, and tax fraud, money laundering and insider trading.

Source: Commerzbank AG (n.d.), "The Business Conduct Guidelines of Commerzbank AG", www.commerzbank.de/en/nachhaltigkeit/governance/governance_1.html

- Implementing legislations or codes of conduct that explicitly prohibit public officials from receiving certain payments or gifts that may create conflict-of-interest situations to their official duty.
- Demanding higher scrutiny for senior officials who have more discretion and decision-making power.

Q11. Are there measures in place to ensure the objectivity and credibility of social, economic and environmental feasibility studies?

Governments could address this issue through:

- Limiting the discretionary scope of public officials in the assessment through:
  - delegating the assessment studies to external experts for social, economic and environmental feasibility studies (see Box 2.29).
  - providing public officials with standardised assessment guidelines.

Box 2.29. **Vadodara Halol Toll Road in India**

The Vadodara Halol Toll Road (VHTR) was one of the first state highway widening projects developed on a public-private partnership basis in India. VHTR was an initiative commissioned as a part of the Vision 2010 – an infrastructure master plan developed by the Government of Gujarat (GoG). The GoG commissioned the Infrastructure Leasing and Financial Services (IL&FS) through a special purpose vehicle (SPV) constituted for this purpose named the Vadodara Halol Toll Road Company Limited (VHTRL). VHTRL in turn appointed a contractor, through international competitive bidding, for the construction, operation and maintenance of the project.

After signing the Memorandum of Agreement, a consulting firm was selected by GoG and IL&FS through a competitive bidding process and commissioned to undertake a preliminary technical, economic feasibility study. Based on the findings of this study, GoG approved widening and strengthening of the existing two-lane road to four lanes with the provision of service roads. Investment recovery was recommended in the form of toll collections.

Source: Ministry of Finance India (n.d.), "Vadodara Halol Toll Road", http://toolkit.pppinindia.com/ports/module3-rocs-vhtr5.php?links=vhtr5 (accessed on 20 October 2015).

- If a consultancy firm is to assess the feasibility of the project, a due diligence check should be carried out prior to the selection, and the selection should be the result of a fair and transparent procurement process.
- Publishing the studies for which the public officials or the experts who carried out the studies will be held responsible.
- Assuring a proper public consultation process associated with the relevant feasibility studies.
- Keeping a record of the assessment of the expert on their report for future reference and penalising those with alleged bias on future public investment project assessments.
- Restricting room for undue influence on the experts through:
  - sanctions on public officials who try to unduly influence the experts' studies
  - carrying out internal concomitant audits and having external scrutiny (see Box 2.30).

Box 2.30. **Public and Private Infrastructure Investment Management Centre (PIMAC) in Korea**

PIMAC is a Korean think tank that conducts project evaluation as preliminary feasibility studies (PFS) and re-assessment studies of feasibility on public investments, and value for money tests for PPP projects of infrastructure investment projects.

The Preliminary Feasibility Studies Guideline provides guidance on how to appraise projects and states what kinds of cost and benefit analysis should be included. The purpose of the guideline is to present results of technical appraisal work logically and clearly, to maintain the consistency across different PFS and to improve the reliability and accountability of the PFS results. It provides for general guidelines and standard guidelines for each area, such as road, railway, airport, harbour, culture, tourism, sports and research and development (R&D).

The guideline includes detailed guidance on economic feasibility, fiscal feasibility assessment, policy analysis (e.g. degree of lagging regional development, promoting regional economy, possibility of receiving fiscal support, consistency with related plans, environmental impact assessment, etc.) and the analytic hierarchy process (AHP).

Source: http://pimac.kdi.re.kr (accessed on 20 October 2015).

Q12. Are there measures in place to limit the influence of a potential private operator of a PPP or a concession?

Governments could address this issue through:

- Establishing standards for risk analysis that limit room for public officials' discretion (see Box 2.31).

Box 2.31. **The risk register, United Kingdom**

The UK Department for Transport requires promoters to construct a comprehensive risk register to mitigate the risk involved in the implementation of large schemes. This register lists the risks that are likely to affect the delivery and operation of the proposed infrastructure. Construction risks (e.g. timescale and cost perspectives) and operational risks (e.g. maintenance risk and revenue risk) and a share of risks associated with climate change should be included in the register. The risk register should identify who owns the risks.

Source: Flyvbjerg, Bent, Massimo Garbuio and Dan Lovallo (2009), "Delusion and deception in large infrastructure projects: Two models for explaining and preventing executive disaster". *California Management Review*, Vol. 51, No. 2.

- Publishing the studies and holding responsible the persons who carried out the report.
- Concomitant, or real-time, audit.
- Providing regulations and sanctions on the use of confidential information by public officials in legislation or in codes of conduct.

3. Planning and document design phase

Clear regulations and legal requirements are helpful to reduce a public official's discretion or avoid private interests from inflicting influence on the process. External scrutiny can be helpful in curbing corruption in the process but sometimes it is not feasible due to limited resources in the public sector. Additionally, it was proposed in a certain country that local contributions to public investment should be required for contractors to increase the sense of responsibility over the investment project. The following questions and answers may provide guidance on how to prevent corrupt practices in this phase.

Q13. Are there measures in place against some actors getting more information as an improper favour?

Governments could address this issue through:

- Digitalising information dissemination (see Box 2.32).
- Establishing sound and comprehensive e-procurement systems for complete dissemination of public procurement information (see Box 2.33).

Q14. Are there measures in place to ensure that the design of the tender documents and specifications are not restrictive or tailored?

Governments could address this issue through:

- Creating an independent assessor commission/committee that will address bidders concerns regarding the design of the tender (see Box 2.34).
- Establishing a tender template limiting over-specification.
- Involving experts groups or individuals to participate/help in the design of the tender documents and specifications to avoid restrictive specifications.
- Ensuring that designs are complete and that a technical commission undertakes site surveys.

Box 2.32. Recommended transparency on major projects, by GIACC

The Global Infrastructure Anti-Corruption Centre (GIACC) suggests that the following information be disclosed for major projects. Information should be provided in a free, easily accessible and comprehensible form, and on a prompt and regular basis.

General project information

(1) name of project owner
(2) structure and principal shareholders of project owner
(3) description, purpose, location of project
(4) project approvals
(5) feasibility and cost-benefit studies
(6) outline specification
(7) original budget
(8) original programme
(9) actual project cost
(10) actual programme
(11) opposition to the project
(12) evaluation reports (interim, final, lifetime).

General funding information

(1) name and address of funder
(2) funding agreement
(3) changes to funding terms
(4) fees paid by/to the funder
(5) funder's cost-benefit/feasibility studies
(6) funder's project evaluation reports
(7) for PFI projects, the financing/user agreement between the public sector user and project owner, changes to this agreement, and reasons for these changes.

Government permit information

For each permit/approval required in relation to this project:

- name, type, purpose
- government department responsible for issuing
- official fee
- official time-scale within which should be issued
- name of official to whom reports can be made.

Major contract information

(1) name of contract
(2) type of procurement procedure
(3) invitations to pre-quality, tender, etc.
(4) list of pre-qualification applicants/tenderers
(5) procurement evaluation report
(6) names of procurement evaluators (to be disclosed after publication of contract award)
(7) name of winning contractor
(8) contractor's principal shareholders
(9) contractor's joint venture members*
(10) contractor's agents*
(11) contract documents
(12) original contract price
(13) original contract scope of work or services
(14) original contract programme
(15) major changes to price, programme and scope of work (i.e. assessed at 5% or more of the original cost or programme) and reasons for these changes
(16) details of any re-award of contract
(17) final contract price
(18) total contract payment
(19) actual programme and completion date
(20) actual scope of work
(21) country where contract payments made
(22) currency of contract payments
(23) contract evaluation reports.

Major sub-contract information

(As for major contracts.)

Independent assessor information

(1) name and qualification of independent assessor
(2) agreement appointing the independent assessor
(3) who nominated the independent assessor
(4) his duty to investigate and report corruption
(5) the contact details of the independent assessor to be used for making reports to him.

Note: *For each Joint Venture Member and Agent, the following should be disclosed: name, principal shareholders, scope of works or services, payment/benefit to be received, country where payment to be made, currency of payment.

Source: GIACC (2008b), "Transparency, Clause 6", www.giaccentre.org/documents/GIACC.PACSPS2Transparency_Nov08_Table2.pdf.

Box 2.33. **Australian Government's procurement information system**

The Australian Government's procurement information system, AusTender, provides centralised publication of Australian Government business opportunities, annual procurement plans, multi-use lists and contracts awarded.

Agencies are required by the Commonwealth Procurement Rules to publish on AusTender standing offer arrangements and contracts with a value of AUD 10 000 or more. Since 2005, Commonwealth Authorities and Companies Act bodies are also required to publish details of certain contracts and standing offers.

On the AusTender website, it is possible to access reports on contract notices, standard offer notices and procurement plans (www.tenders.gov.au/?event=public.reports.list). As an example, the records that are available on line on contract notices include information on the procuring entity, the procurement method, the contract value and period, a description of the contract, and supplier details. The records are searchable by agency, date range, value range, category, confidentiality, supplier name, supplier Australian Business Number (ABN) and report type. It is also possible to download summary records that include information on the total count and value.

Aggregated information that has been extracted from AusTender is available on the website of the Department of Finance.

It includes statistics on:

- total procurement contracts reported, including a breakdown of total value and number of contracts per financial year
- procurement contracts by value threshold, including a breakdown of value, percent of total value, number of contacts and percent of total number of contracts
- small and medium-sized enterprise (SME) participation in procurement
- individual business participation in procurement
- the ratio of goods to services contracts procured
- the top 20 categories for goods and services procurement contracts, including a breakdown of value, percent of total value, and percent of SME participation
- the top 10 procuring Financial Management and Accountability Act 1997 Agencies (FMA), including a breakdown of value, percent of total value, and rank in previous years compared to the most recent ranking.

In addition, the Department of Finance, together with Protiviti, has conducted an analysis of AusTender data for 2010-11 and 2011-12 on: *i)* the split (by value) between the procurement of goods and services by the Australian Government; *ii)* the total value of Australian Government procurement for each United Nations Standard Products and Services Code (UNSPSC) in relation to total expenditure in Australia; *iii)* the total value of goods procured that are likely to be "Australian made" and services procured that are delivered from within Australia; and *iv)* the total value of goods or services procured by the Australian Government that are likely to be imported, in order to determine the impact the Australian Government procurement market has on the Australian economy. The report is available at the Department's website, www.finance.gov.au/procurement/analysis-of-australian-overseas-purchasing-contracts.html.

Source: OECD (forthcoming a), *Compendium of Good Practices for Integrity in Public Procurement*, OECD Publishing, Paris.

Box 2.34. **New York Tappan Zee Hudson River Crossing project: Procurement integrity monitor**

In order to counter the corruption risks associated with the design-build model of the Tappan Zee Bridge project, it was decided to retain an independent procurement integrity monitor for this project. The Governor's office and the New York State Thruway Authority (NYSTA) determined to address the tension between the need, on the one hand, for confidentiality in the evaluation of the proposals and negotiations with the proposers versus, on the other hand, the need for transparency in the decisions surrounding the expenditure of public funds, by having an independent firm, outside of the procurement process itself, monitor compliance with the controls governing that process.

The objectives of the integrity monitor included process evaluation, process enhancements and compliance monitoring. In order to achieve these ends, it was entitled to: *i)* obtain and review selected documentation relating to integrity and security of the procurement process; *ii)* make recommendations for enhancements of the process to appropriate personnel; *iii)* perform monitoring through: unannounced attendance at meetings selected on a random basis; review of documents produced by the procurement process; interview with those involved in process; physical observation of compliance with all critical security/integrity-related controls; communication with appropriate personnel as to any issues found so as to facilitate immediate remediation; and *iv)* prepare a final report.

Source: Thacher Associates (2013), "Tappan Zee Hudson River Crossing Project; Report of the Independent Procurement Integrity Monitor", www.newnybridge.com/documents/int-monitor-report.pdf.

4. Tendering phase

The multiplicity of stakeholders and modes of delivery in this stage opens up many entry points for corruption. Open, transparent and clear criteria for bidding on public contracts (including criteria that potential contractors cannot have been convicted for bribery or corruption or under investigation for bribery or corruption) are essential to guarantee that the procurement process is carried out with integrity. The diversity of the stages makes it unfeasible to have external scrutiny at each stage. Adequate checks and balances in the process are expected in order to ensure the quality of goods and services provided. The following questions and answers may provide guidance on how to prevent corrupt practices in this phase.

Q15. Are there measures in place to ensure the winning bidder is the most qualified?

Governments and business could address this issue through:

- Use of integrity pacts so that government officials and companies adhere to ethical conduct during the procurement process (see Box 2.35).

Box 2.35. **Integrity pacts in India**

Integrity pacts (IPs), developed by Transparency International (TI) in the 1990s, oblige government officials and companies to adhere to ethical conduct. The three main objectives are to enable companies to abstain from corruption by providing assurance to them that competitors will similarly refrain from corruption, and that government agencies are also committed to preventing corruption; governments to reduce the high costs and the distortion effect of corruption in public procurement; and citizens to more easily monitor public decision making and their government's activities.

In the recent past, the Central Vigilance Commission (CVC) has taken commendable initiatives in terms of promoting electronic solutions and integrity pacts. Integrity pacts in procurement help governments, businesses and civil society to fight corruption in the field of public contracting via an agreement on no corruption between the procurement agency and all bidders for a public sector contract. In India, integrity pacts hold additional relevance for the following reasons:

- High ranking in the Corruption Perception Index.
- History of scandals and delays in public procurement.
- Existing anti-corruption regulations have had limited success.

Some 39 public sector companies are using integrity pacts in their procurement process. According to a Transparency International-India document, 96% of Integrity Pact Compliant Public Sector Undertakings feel that the integrity pact has helped in making procurement processes more transparent and 100% feel that the procurement process will not be better off without IP.

Integrity pacts in India have been used in several sectors, such as energy (gas, oil, thermal power), telecommunication or airport construction. In addition, India has developed specific integrity pacts in defence procurement. The Defence Procurement Procedures (DPP) 2006 for the first time introduced a provision called a pre-contract integrity pact, in a move to eliminate "all forms of corruption" in defence deals. The DPP 2006 provided for the appointment of independent monitors (IMs), who would be responsible for examining any violations of the pact, brought to notice by the buyer. However, DPP 2006 did not mention the precise role and power of the IMs. An amendment in 2009 included clauses on the precise role and powers of IMs.

Henceforth, IMs are authorised to scrutinise complaints with regards to violation of integrity pacts, through access to "the relevant office records in connection with the complaints sent to them by the buyer". According to Defence Procurement Procedures 2011, integrity pacts are applicable in procurements worth INR 100 crores (approximately USD 16 million) and above, and in defence enterprises at INR 20 crores (approximately USD 322 000) and above.

Sources: Central Vigilance Commission (2010), "Draft national anti-corruption strategy", http://cvc.nic.in/NationalAntiCorruptionStrategydraft.pdf; Mishra et al. (2012), *Integrity Pact: Assessment of Integrity Pact (IP) in IP Compliant Public Sector Undertakings*, Transparency International, New Delhi, India, www.integritypact.in/download/Assessment%20of%20Integrity%20Pact%20in%20IP%20compliant%20PSUs.pdf

- Implementing an integrity framework (see Box 2.36).

Box 2.36. **PWGSC's Integrity Framework, Canada**

The Public Works and Government Services Canada (PWGSC) has a strong framework in place to support accountability and integrity in its procurement and real property transactions. This includes policies, procedures and governance measures to ensure fairness, openness and transparency.

The key elements of PWGSC's Integrity Framework include the following:

Types of contracts covered: The Integrity Framework only applies to all PWGSC managed contracts and real property transactions, including: construction contracts, goods and services contracts and real property transactions.

Applicability to sub-contractors/sub-lessors: It does not apply to sub-contractors; its relationship is with the prime contractor. However, all procurement instruments or leases stipulate that the contractor agrees to bind the sub-contractor by the same conditions by which the contractor is bound under the contract.

There is no dollar threshold of contracts covered.

Offences covered include, but are not limited to:

Fraud against the government under the Criminal Code of Canada	Fraud under the Financial Administration Act
- Payment of a contingency fee to a person to whom the Lobbying Act applies. - Bribery of judicial officers, public officials or officers. - Suppliers convicted of a listed offence will be ineligible/ debarred for a period of ten years from the date of conviction.	- Corruption, collusion, bid-rigging or any other anti-competitive activity under the Competition Act. - Criminal breach of contract.

Exceptions: The Public Interest Exception applies, on a case-by-case basis, in circumstances in which it is necessary to the public interest to enter into business with a supplier that has been convicted or has been conditionally or absolutely discharged of an offence under PWGSC's provisions. Possible circumstances necessary to the public interest could include:

- No other supplier is capable of performing the contract.
- An emergency.
- National security.
- Health and safety.
- Economic harm.

In such cases, PWGSC could also impose additional stringent controls, administrative measures, and monitoring in the contract or real property agreement.

Recourse in the event of a conviction post contract award: PWGSC may terminate a contract or real property agreement for default if a conviction occurs post contract award, or may continue with the option to impose oversight and monitoring measures.

List of ineligible suppliers: PWGSC does not maintain a list of ineligible suppliers:

- By bidding, suppliers certify that they do not have any of the convictions or have pleaded guilty and have been absolutely or conditionally discharged of offences under PWGSC's Integrity Framework.

PWGSC verifies the eligibility of suppliers and authorises them for the specific transaction.

Source: Public Works and Government Services Canada (2015), "Government of Canada's Integrity Regime", www.tpsgc-pwgsc.gc.ca/ci-if/ci-if-eng.html.

- Providing verbal debriefing by the government to aggrieved bidders to provide a better understanding of how the decision was reached, increasing understanding of the integrity involved in the process (see Box 2.37).

Box 2.37. **Verbal debriefing in the United Kingdom**

Verbal debriefing is a recognised good practice that many OECD member countries use to promote a constructive and transparent dialogue with the marketplace and expand their supply base. In addition, by giving unsuccessful suppliers more insight into the process, they can better understand how the decision was reached, increasing the understanding of the integrity involved in the process. More importantly, it also serves as an additional motivation to encourage procurement officers to conduct procedures appropriately and according to integrity safeguards.

The UK regulations require departments to debrief candidates in contracts exceeding European thresholds. They also strongly recommend verbal debriefing in contracts below thresholds, which is the responsibility of the contracting agency or public organisation.

Debriefing discussions –face to face, over the telephone or by videoconference – are held within a maximum of 15 days following the award of the contract. Sessions are chaired by senior procurement personnel who have been involved in the procurement.

The topics for discussion during the verbal debriefing depend mainly on the nature of the procurement. However, the session follows a predefined structure. First, after introductions are made, the procurement selection and evaluation process is explained openly. The second stage concentrates on the strengths and weaknesses of the supplier's bid. After the discussion, the suppliers are asked to describe their views on the process and raise any further concerns or questions. More importantly, at all stages it remains forbidden to reveal information about other submissions. Following the debriefing, a note of the meeting is made for the record.

An important result of an effective debriefing is that it reduces the likelihood of a legal challenge because it proves to suppliers that the process has been carried out correctly and according to rules of procurement and probity. Although the causality between the introduction of detailed debriefings and legal reviews cannot be proven, a sharp decrease in the number of reviews was observed in the United Kingdom between 1995 and 2005 (from approximately 3 000 to 1 200).

Source: OECD (2013), *Public Procurement Review of the Mexican Institute of Social Security: Enhancing Efficiency and Integrity for Better Health Care*, OECD Public Governance Reviews, OECD Publishing, Paris, http://dx.doi.org/10.1787/9789264197480-en.

- Inviting civil society to monitor the process to ensure that it is carried out in a transparent manner (e.g. use of social witnesses) (see Box 2.38).

Box 2.38. Social witnesses in Mexico

Since 2009, social witnesses are required to participate in all stages of public tendering procedures above certain thresholds as a way to promote public scrutiny. In 2014, these thresholds were MXN 336 million (approximately USD 25 million) for goods and services and MXN 672 million (approximately USD 50 million) for public works.

Social witnesses are non-government organisations and individuals selected by the Ministry of Public Administration (SFP) through public tendering. SFP keeps a registry of the approved social witnesses and evaluates their performance; unsatisfactory performance potentially results in their removal from the registry.

When a federal entity requires the involvement of a social witness, it informs SFP who designates one from the registry.

As of January 2014, SFP had registered 39 social witnesses for public procurement projects, 5 civil society organisations and 34 individuals. This number has grown from 5 social witnesses in 2005 to 40 later in 2014.

SFP notes that "the monitoring of the most relevant procurement processes of the federal government through social witnesses has had an impact in improving procurement procedures by virtue of their contributions and experience, to the point that they have become a strategic element for ensuring the transparency and credibility of the procurement system." An OECD-World Bank Institute study (2006) indicates that the participation of social witnesses in the procurement processes of the Federal Electricity Commission (*Comisión Federal de Electricidad*) created savings of approximately USD 26 million in 2006 and increased the number of bidders by over 50%.

Source: OECD (2013a), *Public Procurement Review of the Mexican Institute of Social Security: Enhancing Efficiency and Integrity for Better Health Care*, OECD Public Governance Reviews, OECD Publishing, Paris, http://dx.doi.org/10.1787/9789264197480-en.

- Ensuring that a review and remedy system is in place that has the following characteristics:
  - provides timely redress
  - is effective in correcting (and thus preventing) instances of unlawfulness on the part of economic operators and/or contracting authorities
  - is transparent and clear (i.e. understandable and easy to use by economic operators)
  - is non-discriminatory and available to all the bidders wishing to participate in a specific contract award procedure (see Box 2.39).

Box 2.39. The Office for Government Procurement Review in Japan

The Japanese system of complaints concerning government procurement of goods and services (including construction services) aims to ensure greater transparency, fairness, and competitiveness in the government procurement system, under the principle of non-discrimination of foreign and domestic sources.

The Government Procurement Review Board (the Board) composed of 7 committee members and 16 special members receives and reviews complaints. The Office of Government Procurement Review (OGPR), headed by the Chief Cabinet Secretary and with administrative vice ministers or directors from all ministries and agencies as its members is also notified of review procedures. Persons or bodies wishing to file a complaint may do so with the Board within ten days after the basis of the complaint is known. The Board will examine complaints received within seven working days of filing and determine whether they will be accepted for review.

If a complaint is accepted for review, the Board will immediately notify the complainant, OGPR, and the procuring entity of this in writing and publicly announce its decision through the Official Gazette, the Internet (www5.cao.go.jp/access/english/kouji-e.html), and other means, soliciting the attendance of participants interested in the complaint. The procuring entity is required to present a report to the Board; if the complainant or the participants disagree with this report, they may present statements to the Board or request a review by the Board, which the Board will subsequently undertake. Finally, a report on findings will be drawn up within 90 days by the Board in cases of standard review. This period can be shortened if the complainant or the procuring entity so desire. This time limit may also vary according to the type of procurement of the complaint. If the Board finds that procurement has been carried out in a manner inconsistent with any provision of the Agreement on Government Procurement or other applicable measures, it will draw up recommendations.

Source: OECD (forthcoming a), *Compendium of Good Practices for Integrity in Public Procurement*, OECD Publishing, Paris.

- Carrying out a parallel independent procurement evaluation to strengthen the detection of collusion, bid-rigging and favouring a supplier (see Box 2.40).

Box 2.40. The US Government Accountability Office's increased role as a review and remedy body

The laws and regulations that govern contracting with the federal government are designed to ensure that federal procurements are conducted fairly. On occasion, bidders or others interested in government procurements may have reason to believe that a contract has been, or is about to be, awarded improperly or illegally, or that they have been unfairly denied a contract or an opportunity to compete for a contract. A major avenue of relief for those concerned about the propriety of an award has been the Government Accountability Office (GAO) (formerly known as the General Accounting Office).

A bid protest is an adjudicative process; it is not an audit conducted by GAO's audit team in accordance with generally accepted government audit standards. Moreover, unlike GAO audit reports, a GAO bid protest decision does not address broad programmatic issues, such as whether a weapons programme is being managed effectively and within cost, nor does a GAO bid protest decision evaluate which company's proposal is better.

Box 2.40. **The US Government Accountability Office's increased role as a review and remedy body** *(continued)*

Over the years, GAO has developed a substantial body of law and standard procedures for considering bid protests.

For more than 80 years (the first bid protest decision was published by GAO in 1926), GAO has provided an objective, independent, and impartial forum for the resolution of disputes concerning the awards of federal contracts. Over the years, the decisions of the Comptroller General of the United States, the head of GAO, in bid protest cases have resulted in a uniform body of law applicable to the procurement process upon which the Congress, the courts, agencies, and the public rely. Although protesters may be represented by counsel, filing a bid protest with GAO is easy and inexpensive and does not require the services of an attorney. In addition, matters can usually be resolved more quickly by protests filed with GAO than by court litigation.

Filing a GAO protest may trigger an automatic stay of contract award or performance that lasts for the duration of the protest. Such automatic stays are unique to bid protests filed with GAO and help account for GAO's popularity as a protest forum. Agencies may, however, override these stays upon determining that urgent and compelling circumstances will not permit waiting for GAO's decision, or performance of the contract is in the best interests of the United States.

Timeline of a bid protest

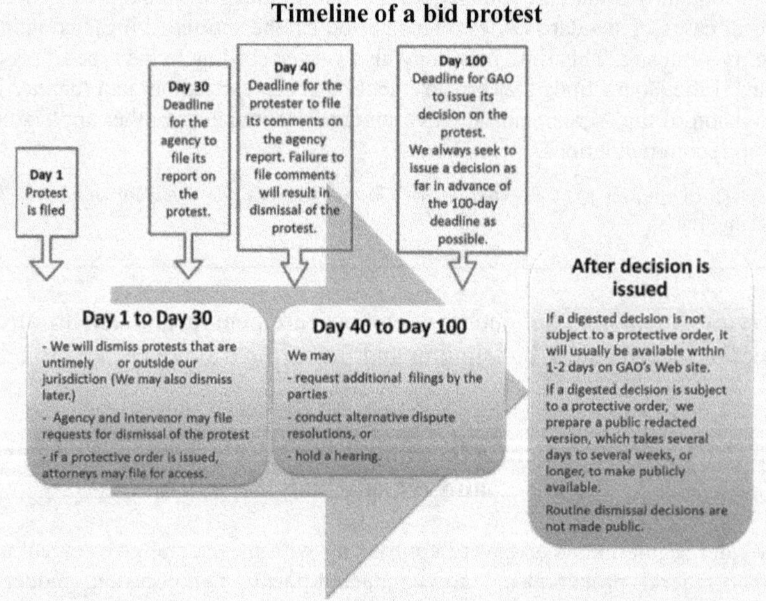

Source: United States Government Accountability Office (2009), "Bid Protests at GAO: A Descriptive Guide", Ninth Edition, GAO-09-471SP, Washington, DC, www.gao.gov/assets/210/203631.pdf; www.gao.gov/legal/bids/timeline.html (accessed on 20 October 2015).

Q16. Are there measures in place to assure the integrity of bidding companies?

Governments could require all bidders on a contract to produce independent certification as a pre-qualification requirement, or specify the necessity to comply with certain standards to participate in the bidding process (see Boxes 2.41 and 2.42).

Box 2.41. **British Standard BS 10500**

BSI Standards is the United Kingdom's National Standards Body. It is the UK representative at the International Organization for Standardization (ISO). BS 10500 is intended to help an organisation to implement an effective anti-bribery management system. It can be used both in the United Kingdom and internationally. The requirements of UK law and internationally recognised good practice are taken into account. It is applicable to small, medium and large organisations in the public, private and voluntary sectors.

BS 10500 is likely to be useful to organisations in the following way:

- It will help provide assurance to the board and shareholders of an organisation that their organisation has implemented best practice anti-bribery controls.
- A project developer or project funder may require the contractors, suppliers and consultants which are constructing a project to provide certification to BS 10500 as evidence that they have implemented anti-bribery controls in their organisations.
- Organisations may require their major sub-contractors, suppliers and consultants to provide evidence of certification to BS 10500 as part of their supply chain approval process (on a similar basis to their requiring evidence of certification to ISO 9001, etc.).

In order to comply with BS 10500, an organisation must implement the requirements featured under these categories:

1. Anti-bribery policy
2. Anti-bribery management system (ABMS)
3. Communicating the anti-bribery policy and ABMS
4. Education, training and/or guidance
5. Compliance manager
6. Risk assessment
7. Due diligence
8. Implementation of ABMS by controlled organisations and business associates
9. Employment procedures
10. Gifts, hospitality, donations and similar benefits
11. Facilitation payments
12. Delegated decision making
13. Anti-bribery contract terms
14. Financial controls
15. Procurement and other commercial controls
16. Raising concerns
17. Investigating and dealing with bribery
18. Documenting the ABMS
19. Monitoring and reviewing the ABMS
20. Improvement of the ABMS

Source: GIACC (2012), "British Standard BS 10500", www.giaccentre.org/documents/GIACC.WEBSITE.BS10500.SUMMARY.pdf

Box 2.42. **ISO 37001: An anti-bribery management systems standard**

ISO 37001 is a proposed new anti-bribery management systems standard that is currently under development by the International Organization for Standardization (ISO). Over 80 experts, from 28 participating countries, 16 observer countries and 7 liaison organisations, are involved in the drafting of the standard. The draft is currently at Committee Draft 2 stage. The timetable envisages publication of the standard in late 2016.

ISO 37001 is designed to help an organisation implement an anti-bribery management system. It specifies a series of measures that the organisation should implement to help the organisation prevent, detect and address bribery, and provides guidance in relation to their implementation. ISO 37001 is designed to be used by small, medium and large organisations in the public, private and voluntary sectors. It is a flexible tool, which can be adapted according to the size and nature of the organisation and the bribery risk it faces.

ISO 37001 requires the organisation to implement a series of measures in a proportionate and reasonable manner. These include adopting an anti-bribery policy, requiring top management leadership, appointing a person to oversee anti-bribery compliance, providing training to personnel, undertaking bribery risk assessments and due diligence on projects and business associates, and implementing financial and commercial controls, and reporting and investigation procedures.

Source: International Organization for Standardization (2015), "ISO 37001 anti-bribery management systems standard: Summary FAQ", http://www.iso.org/iso/iso_37001_anti-bribery_management_systems_standard_brochure.pdf

Q17. Are there measures in place to prevent bid rigging, collusion or the agree sharing of the market or future contracts in a public investment?

Governments could address this issue through:

- Using framework agreements created through competitive processes.
- Using a pre-qualification system with the adequate technical, financial and qualitative criteria. The pre-qualification phase could include a background check on previous corruption offenses.
- Using a two-envelope approach whereby the envelope containing the price is only considered following a technical evaluation (see Box 2.43).

Box 2.43. **Two-envelope system used in the bids submission phase in the Slovak Republic**

Two substantial amendments to the Act No. 25/2006 Coll., on Public Procurement became effective in 2013. In the bids submission phase of the procurement cycle, the one-stage tender process has been replaced by a two-stage tender, involving a "two envelope system".

Bids in the tenders are to be submitted in two parts: the "Criteria" part contains the offer with respect to the award criteria, i.e. in most cases only the price; while the "Other" part contains all other documentation and information related to the bid. The "Other" part is opened first and only after evaluation of whether the selection criteria (e.g. technical equipment) have been met can the "Criteria" part of all submitted bids be opened and evaluated. Generally, such a two stage process should ensure that the price does not influence the technical evaluation of the bid.

Source: Schoenherr (2013b), "Slovakia: Substantial changes in public procurement - Every detail counts", www.schoenherr.eu/knowledge/knowledge-detail/slovakia-substantial-changes-in-public-procurement-every-detail-counts/.

Q18. Are there measures in place to ensure that non-competitive procedures are not used without proper justification?

Governments could address this issue through:

- Clearly defining and disseminating legal requirements for the use of a non-competitive procedure.
- Ensuring that all the justifications are properly presented, and make them public.
- Ensuring that this type of decision is not at the discretion of one individual (e.g. Four-eyes Principle) (see Box 2.44).

Box 2.44. **The Four-eyes Principle: Tappan Zee Bridge Project, New York State**

The four-eye principle is a requirement that two individuals review and approve some action before it can be taken. For the construction of the Tappan Zee Bridge in the State of New York, several teams were set up to ensure the respect of the "four-eyes" principle and the fairness of the selection process during the procurement phase:

- A Procurement Management Team, comprised of a team of public and private employees, responsible for directing the overall evaluation and selection process. A Legal Team, comprised of public and private legal advisors to conduct a legal pass/fail analysis of aspects of the proposals and provide guidance throughout the procurement process.
- A Financial Team to perform a financial pass/fail review and a net present value analysis of the price proposals.
- A Price Reasonableness Team to conduct reviews of each of the proposals and provide recommendations to the BRSC regarding the reasonableness of the pricing for each of the proposals.
- A Technical Evaluation Teams to evaluate the technical strengths and weaknesses of each proposal.
- A Value Assessment Team comprised of engineers and other professionals from both the public and private sectors, to assemble all of the reports for each proposer, and where feasible, use the accumulated reports to quantify the technical strengths and weaknesses of each proposal.
- A Blue Ribbon Selection Committee to present a non-binding recommendation to the Selection Executives. A Bridge Design Aesthetic Team, comprised of artists and architects, to review the proposed bridge designs and assist in the evaluation process.
- A group of Selection Executives comprised of the members of the Major Projects Committee of the Thruway Authority's Board, to review the selection and findings of the BRSC. The ultimate determination to award a contract was made by the full NYSTA Board.

Source: Thacher Associates (2013), "Tappan Zee Hudson River Crossing Project; Report of the Independent Procurement Integrity Monitor", www.newnybridge.com/documents/int-monitor-report.pdf.

5. Implementation and contract management phase

Q19. Are there measures in place to ensure that no false reporting of invoices regarding costs associated to materials, labour hours and qualifications of staff takes place?

Governments could address this issue through:

- Publicising the estimated cost of the project and the final cost incurred to citizens through media and community groups.

- Ensuring that profit and labour costs are separated from the rates for materials and equipment.
- Increasing the functionalities of the e-procurement systems to cover the contract management phase and assure publication of relevant information in informational portals, including variations and reasons for the overrun (see Box 2.45).

Box 2.45. **Integrated e-procurement system: KONEPS in Korea**

In Korea, a notable improvement has been made in the transparency of public procurement administration since the early 2000s through the implementation of a national e-procurement system.

In 2002, Public Procurement Service (PPS), the central procurement agency of Korea, introduced a fully integrated, end-to-end e-procurement system called KONEPS (Korean ON-line E-Procurement System). This system covers the entire procurement cycle electronically (including a one-time registration, tendering, contracts, inspection and payment) and related documents are exchanged on line. KONEPS links with about 140 external systems to share and retrieve any necessary information, and provide a one-stop service, including automatic collection of bidder's qualification data, delivery report, e-invoicing and e-payment. Furthermore, it provides related information on a real-time basis.

All public organisations are mandated to publish tenders through KONEPS. In 2012, over 62.7% of Korea's total public procurement (USD 106 billion) was conducted through KONEPS. In KONEPS 45 000 public entities interact with 244 000 registered suppliers. According to PPS, the system has boosted efficiency in procurement, and significantly reduced transaction costs. In addition, the system has increased participation in public tenders and has considerably improved transparency, eliminating instances of corruption by preventing illegal practices and collusive acts. For example, the Korea Fair Trade Commission runs on KONEPS, the Korean BRIAS system which is the automated detection system for detecting suspicious bid strategies. According to the integrity assessment conducted by Korea Anti-Corruption and Civil Rights Commission, the Integrity Perception Index of PPS has improved from 6.8 to 8.52 out of 10 as the highest score, since the launch of KONEPS.

A key concern for illegal practices was borrowed e-certificates. In order to mitigate this risk, the Public Procurement Service introduced "Fingerprint Recognition E-bidding" in 2010. In the Fingerprint Recognition E-bidding system, each user can tender for only one company by using a biometric security token. Fingerprint information is stored only in the concerned supplier's file, thus avoiding any controversy over the government's storage of personal biometric information. By July 2010, it was applied in all tenders carried out via the KONEPS by local governments and other public organisations procuring goods, services and construction projects. In 2011, PPS launched a new bidding service allowing the bidding process to take place via smartphones through newly developed security tokens and applications.

Source: OECD (2013b), *Implementing the OECD Principles for Integrity in Public Procurement: Progress since 2008*, OECD Publishing, Paris, http://dx.doi.org/10.1787/9789264201385-en.

Q20. Are there measures in place to ensure that there is no delay in public investment due to corrupt practices?

Governments could address this issue through:

- Creating a website that monitors the advancement of the public investment in real time and how its advancement compares to the cost and time estimations.
- Providing tools to enable citizens to exercise public oversight of the public investment (Box 2.46).

Box 2.46. Public Oversight of Infrastructure in Colombia

Rolling on the Road

Rolling on the Road (*Rodando la Vía*) is an initiative fostered by the Transparency Secretariat that aims to enhance public oversight of road infrastructure projects. It was developed following the signing of the Pact for Transparency of the Infrastructure Sector (*Pacto por la Transparencia del Sector de Infraestructura*) in May 2015 by several entities of the national government and by more than 70 local authorities.

The initiative requires the inspectors of said projects to upload – on the internet – videos of the works in progress, from beginning to end of the road. This tool allows citizens to oversee the development of the public infrastructure projects and to raise complaints in case they identify wrong use of resources. The videos uploaded during the first phase of the initiative (July through December of 2015) reach nearly 263 miles of road infrastructure projects, distributed along seven Colombian regions (*departamentos*).

An example of aforementioned videos can be found at the following link: www.youtube.com/watch?v=gPk1-cSdoTk&list=PLilxNbN_Bml0nDmsHbAdwAFt-ErzSoCTW&index=3.

White Elephants

In 2014 the Transparency Secretariat launched the app White Elephants, which allows citizens to report any type of unfinished infrastructure projects. The app allows any person to take pictures of a white elephant with a smartphone and report its location. The reports are gathered by the Transparency Secretariat, which assesses each case and impulses legal actions aimed at the recovery of assets and punishment of liable persons.

Source: Presidential Transparency Secretariat, Colombia.

- Training community monitors to observe the progress and quality of the project (see Box 2.47).

Box 2.47. Online tracking of public works in Mexico and Chile

The State's Employees' Social Security and Social Services Institute in Mexico implemented a portal on the procurement of public works. This portal was developed by the Control and Supervision of Works at a Distance (COSODI) unit, as a new model of control and audit for public works. COSODI carries out risk analyses and internal assessments, and develops monitoring tools throughout the procurement cycle (planning to execution) to ensure the proper completion of works, and detect risks of fraud and corruption. The portal provides real-time, accurate information on the awarded public works procurement, thus providing an opportunity for society at large to monitor the progress made in conducting the works. The website provides information on the type of contract awarded, the period during which it should be implemented, the geographic location and the status of implementation and the financial payments. The portal also provides comparative data on the total value of works contracted by the state.

Box 2.47. **Online tracking of public works in Mexico and Chile** *(continued)*

Chile's Supreme Audit Institution, the Comptroller General of the Republic of Chile (*Contraloría General de la República*, CGR), is established by the Constitution as an autonomous government body. Infrastructure investment is a main category of the CGR's *ex post* audit function, which focuses on the technical and administrative activities of public sector entities responsible for public works, the coherence of public procurement processes, the proportionality and justification of any changes to original objectives and legal and regulatory compliance of the entity.

In December 2014, the CGR launched the GEO-CGR portal that stores and allows for the publication, articulation and consultation of geo-referenced information on the investment of resources in public works, with the aim of promoting social control by providing citizens and other users with the tools to monitor reliably, in a timely fashion, and to categorise information by territory. Users can lodge complaints and make suggestions on control, facilitating the easier and active participation of citizens in ensuring control in the public sector.

Sources: OECD (2013a), *Public Procurement Review of the Mexican Institute of Social Security: Enhancing Efficiency and Integrity for Better Health Care*, OECD Public Governance Reviews, OECD Publishing, Paris, http://dx.doi.org/10.1787/9789264197480-en; OECD (forthcoming b), Progress in Chile's Supreme Audit Institution: Reforms, Outreach and Impact, OECD Publishing, Paris.

6. Evaluation and audit phase

Evaluation and auditing of public investment projects reaffirms its significance when considering its role in delivering public policy goals. In this vein, the evaluation and audit phase of a public investment project can also partially assess the achievements of the government in delivering public policy goals.

Given the importance of the audit function for integrity throughout the investment project cycle, operational independence is critical, from the appointment of institutional leadership to the enforcement of codes of conduct at all levels. As autonomous entities, audit institutions must also be protected from external and undue influence and empowered with the appropriate resources to fulfil their function.

In this process, accountability of the auditors carries a significant weight and relying on their discretion alone can be insufficient in some contexts. Their accountability can be strengthened through adequate legal framework on their probity. To complement it, regulations and sanctions should also be in place against those who may try to exert undue influence on auditors. The following questions and answers may provide guidance on how to prevent corrupt practices in this phase.

Q21. Are there measures in place to ensure that the entities (public or private) have an effective system of internal controls and financial reporting to monitor and identify irregularities?

Governments could address this issue through:

- Application of the Committee of Sponsoring Organisations of the Treadway Commission (COSO) Framework on internal control (establishment of a control environment, appropriate risk assessment, establishment of control activities, clear information and communication throughout the entity, and monitoring of control mechanisms for their effectiveness and appropriateness). In particular, a few requirements stand out:

- There exists an appropriate application of robust risk assessment procedures (for example, integrated financial risk assessments).
- There is a clear procedure for dealing with unexpected risks, and mechanisms through which auditors can seek advice and recourse.
- An appropriate level of risk tolerance is established by entity management and communicated clearly to internal audit as well as to all staff of the entity (see Box 2.48).

- Ensuring that financial transactions are adequately identified and recorded (i.e. no "off the books" expenditures or non-identified accounts).
- Monitoring cash payments or payments in kind.
- Ensuring information is kept for sufficient period and not prematurely destroyed (OECD, UNODC, World Bank, 2013).
- Cross-referencing public expenditure information to detect irregularities within and across sectors (see Box 2.49).

Box 2.48. **International standards on internal control and audit: COSO Framework**

The international industry standard on internal control, as espoused by the Committee of Sponsoring Organisations of the Treadway Commission (COSO), articulates the components of effective internal control as involving the following elements: the control environment, risk assessment, control activities, information and communication, and monitoring activities. All these elements are essential and must be able to operate together seamlessly for an effective internal control system.

Component	Principles
1. Control environment	
• Established by senior management • Set of standards, processes and structures • Represents integrity and ethical values of the organisation • Enables management oversight • Processes to ensure a competent workforce • Performance measures, incentives and rewards	1. Demonstrates commitment to integrity and ethical values 2. Exercises oversight responsibility 3. Establishes structure, authority and responsibility 4. Demonstrates commitment to competence 5. Enforces accountability
2. Risk assessment	
• Dynamic and iterative process • Establishes risk tolerance against clear organisational objectives	6. Specifies relevant objectives 7. Identifies and analyses risk 8. Assesses fraud risk 9. Identifies and analyses significant change
3. Control activities	
• Performed at all levels of an entity • May be preventative or detective	10. Selects and develops control activities 11. Selects and develops general controls over technology 12. Deploys through policies and procedures
4. Information and communication	
• Using relevant quality information to carry out internal control responsibilities • Continual, iterative process of providing, sharing and obtaining necessary information	13. Uses relevant information 14. Communicates internally 15. Communicates externally
5. Monitoring activities	
• Scope and frequency partly depends on assessment of risks and management considerations	16. Conducts ongoing and/or separate evaluations 17. Evaluates and communicates deficiencies

Source: Adapted from COSO (2013), "COSO's Internal Control – Integrated Framework, Executive Summary", May, www.coso.org/documents/990025P_Executive_Summary_final_may20_e.pdf COSO (2012), "An Update of COSO's Internal Control – Integrated Framework", May, www.coso.org/documents/cosoicifoutreachdeck_05%2018%2012.pdf

Box 2.49. **Public Spending Observatory in Brazil**

The Office of the Comptroller General of the Union launched the Public Spending Observatory (*Observatório da Despesa Pública*) in 2008 as the basis for continuous detection and sanctioning of misconduct and corruption. Through the Public Spending Observatory, procurement expenditure data are cross-checked with other government databases as a means of identifying atypical situations that, while not *a priori* evidence of irregularities, warrant further examination.

Based on the experience over the past several years, a number of daily actions are taken to cross-check procurement and other government data. This exercise generates "orange" or "red" flags that can be followed up and investigated by officials within the Office of the Comptroller General of the Union. In many cases, follow-up activities are conducted together with special advisors on internal control and internal audit units within public organisations.

Examples of these tracks related to procurement and administrative contracts include possible conflicts of interest, inappropriate use of exemptions and waivers and substantial contract amendments. A number of tracks also relate to suspicious patterns of bid-rotation and market division among competitors by sector, geographic area or time, which might indicate that bidders are acting in a collusive scheme.

Finally, tracks also exist regarding the use of federal government payment cards and administrative agreements (*convenios*). In 2013, there were 60 000 instances of warnings originated from the computer-assisted audit tracks used by the Office of the Comptroller General of the Union to identify possible procurement irregularities, like:

- business relations between suppliers participating in the same procurement procedure
- personal relations between suppliers and public officials in procurement procedures
- fractioning of contracts in order to use exemptions to the competitive procurement modality
- use of bid waiver when more than one "exclusive" supplier exists
- non-compliance by suppliers with tender submission deadlines
- bid submission received prior to publication of a procurement notice
- registration of bid submissions on non-working days
- possibility of competition in exemptions
- supplier's bid submissions or company records with the same registered address
- participation of newly established suppliers in procurement procedures
- contract amounts above the legally prescribed ceiling for the procurement modality used
- contract amendments above an established limit, in violation of the specific tender modality
- contract amendments within a month of contract award, in violation of the specific tender modality
- commitments issued prior to the original proposal date in the commitment registration system
- evidence of bidder rotation in procurement procedures
- bidding procedures involving suppliers registered in the Information Registry of Unpaid Federal Public Sector Credits (*Cadastro Informativo de Créditos Não Quitados do Setor Público Federal*).*
- use of reverse auctions for engineering services
- micro- and small enterprises linked to other enterprises
- micro- and small enterprises with shareholders in other micro- and small enterprises
- micro- and small enterprises with earnings greater than BRL 0.24 million or BRL 2.40 million, respectively.

Source: OECD (2012), *OECD Integrity Review of Brazil: Managing Risks for a Cleaner Public Service*, OECD Public Governance Reviews, OECD Publishing, http://dx.doi.org/10.1787/9789264119321-en.

Q22. Are there measures in place to guarantee the independence of auditing institution or auditors?

Governments could address this issue through:

- Ensuring that auditors are subject to specific codes of conduct regarding their contacts with contractors (see Box 2.50).

Box 2.50. **The International Organisation of Supreme Audit Institutions' Code of Ethics for auditors in the public sector**

The International Organisation of Supreme Audit Institutions (INTOSAI) developed a Code of Ethics for auditors in the public sector. The independence, powers and responsibilities place high ethical demands on their daily conduct, which should be beyond reproach in all circumstances. The Code of Ethics is structured around five key areas:

1. Promulgation of trust, confidence and credibility

The conduct of public sector auditors should be beyond reproach and worthy of trust of its stakeholders, who should also be assured of the fairness, impartiality, accuracy and reliability of audit work.

2. Integrity

Public sector auditors have a duty to adhere to high standards of behaviour in the course of their work and in their relationships with staff of audited entities. Integrity requires auditors to conduct audit work in line with principles of objectivity and impartiality and to make decisions with the public interest in mind.

3. Independence, objectivity and impartiality

Public Sector Auditors should strive to be independent from audited entities and interested groups, and free from interference of political or personal interests. This means that auditors should focus on topics under review and should express conclusions in opinions based exclusively on evidence obtained and assembled in accordance with their entity's auditing standards.

4. Professional secrecy

Public sector auditors should not disclose information that is gathered throughout the audit cycle to third parties in writing or orally, which is not part of its statutory or legal responsibilities which form their normal proceedings.

5. Competence

Public sector auditors have a duty to conduct themselves in a professional manner in carrying out their work, and should not undertake work that they are not competent to perform. This coincides with the auditor's full understanding and application of auditing, accounting and financial management standards, policies, procedures and practices as well as constitutional and legal frameworks.

Source: INTOSAI (n.d.), "Code of Ethics, International Standards of Supreme Audit Institutions (ISSAI 30)".

- Excluding auditing institutions from future public investment audits if they are found complicit in wrongdoings (e.g. receiving bribes, using false information in their reports).
- Creating specialised oversight bodies to apply strict procedures for controlling costs and monitoring progress to ensure that projects were built on time and within budget.
- There is control of the controllers – e.g. internal audit is overseen by external audit, which is in turn overseen by another objective external body.

Q23. Do audit functions have adequate capacity and resources to provide timely and reliable audits, as well as to remain insulated from manipulation of audit processes?

Governments could assist by:

- Ensuring that audit functions are adequately resourced.
- Establishing systems and databases on which auditees can draw reliable information about ongoing public works.
- Promulgating technical skills to employ innovative technological advancements that ensure more reliable audits and data.

Bibliography

APEC (Asia-Pacific Economic Cooperation) (n.d.), "Anti-corruption Code of Conduct for Business", www.apec.org/Groups/SOM-Steering-Committee-on-Economic-and-Technical-Cooperation/Task-Groups/~/media/Files/Groups/ACT/%2007_act_codebrochure.ashx (accessed on 20 October 2015).

BP (British Petroleum) (n.d.), "Our code of conduct", www.bp.com/en/global/corporate/sustainability/how-we-operate/our-code-of-conduct.html

Butcher, L. (2014), "Aviation; London Heathrow Airport", *Commons Briefing Papers,* SN01136, http://researchbriefings.parliament.uk/ResearchBriefing/Summary/ SN01136.

Central Vigilance Commission (2010), "Draft national anti-corruption strategy", http://cvc.nic.in/NationalAntiCorruptionStrategydraft.pdf.

Commerzbank AG (n.d.), "The Business Conduct Guidelines of Commerzbank AG", https://www.commerzbank.de/en/nachhaltigkeit/governance/governance_1.html.

COSO (2013), "COSO's Internal Control – Integrated Framework, Executive Summary", May, www.coso.org/documents/990025P_Executive_Summary_final_may20_e.pdf

COSO (2012), "An Update of COSO's Internal Control – Integrated Framework", May, www.coso.org/documents/cosoicifoutreachdeck_05%2018%2012.pdf

CoST (Construction Sector Transparency Initiative) (2013), "Establishing a multi-stakeholder group and national secretariat", www.constructiontransparency.org/documentdownload.axd?documentresourceid=29.

European Commission (n.d.), "Transparency Register", http://ec.europa.eu/ transparencyregister/public/homePage.do?redir=false&locale=en.

Flyvbjerg, B., M. Garbuio and D. Lovallo (2009), "Delusion and deception in large infrastructure projects: Two models for explaining and preventing executive disaster". *California Management Review*, Vol. 51, No. 2.

GIACC (Global Infrastructure Anti-Corruption Centre) (2012), "British Standard BS 10500", www.giaccentre.org/documents/GIACC.WEBSITE.BS10500.SUMMARY.pdf

GIACC (2008a), "Examples of corruption in infrastructure", www.giaccentre.org/documents/GIACC.CORRUPTIONEXAMPLES.pdf.

GIACC (2008b), "Transparency, Clause 6", www.giaccentre.org/documents/ GIACC.PACSPS2Transparency_Nov08_.Table2.pdf.

Government of the Republic of the Philippines (2014), "Procurement of Infrastructure Projects: BICOL International Airport Development Project", www.dotc.gov.ph/images/Public_Bidding/CivilWorks/Air_Sector/2014/NewLegazpi Apt--BIADP_P2a/BidDocs_BIADP_Pkg2A_Clean_WithEdits_SGD.pdf.

Government of South Australia (2013), "Code of Practice for the South Australian Construction Industry", Department of Planning, Transport and Infrastructure, www.infrastructure.sa.gov.au/BuildingManagement/policies.

Government of South Australia (n.d.), "DPTI Procurement Practices and Policies", www.dpti.sa.gov.au/open_government/proactive_disclosure/details_of_procurement_practices_within_departments.

INTOSAI (International Organisation of Supreme Audit Institutions) (n.d.), "Code of Ethics, International Standards of Supreme Audit Institutions (ISSAI 30)".

ISO (International Organization for Standardization) (2015), "ISO 37001 anti-bribery management systems standard: Summary FAQ", www.iso.org/iso/iso_37001_anti-bribery_management_systems_standard_brochure.pdf.

Ministry of Finance India (n.d.), "Vadodara Halol Toll Road", http://toolkit.pppinindia.com/ports/module3-rocs-vhtr5.php?links=vhtr5 (accessed on 20 October 2015).

New Zealand State Services Commission (2007), "Standards of Integrity and Conduct", www.ssc.govt.nz/sites/all/files/Code-of-conduct-StateServices.pdf.

OECD (forthcoming a), *Compendium of Good Practices for Integrity in Public Procurement,* OECD Publishing, Paris.

OECD (forthcoming b), *Progress of Chile's Supreme Audit Institution: Reforms, outreach and impact*, OECD Publishing, Paris.

OECD (forthcoming c), "The governance of public infrastructure – Towards a whole-of-government perspective", internal working paper.

OECD (2016), *Financing Democracy: Funding of Political Parties and Election Campaigns and the Risk of Policy Capture,* OECD Public Governance Reviews, OECD Publishing, Paris. http://dx.doi.org/10.1787/9789264249455-en.

OECD (2015a), "Recommendation of the Council on Public Procurement", www.oecd.org/gov/ethics/OECD-Recommendation-on-Public-Procurement.pdf.

OECD (2015b), "Implementation toolkit: Effective public investment across levels of government", www.oecd.org/effective-public-investment-toolkit/public-investment.htm.

OECD (2015c), *Policy guidance for Investment in Clean Energy Infrastructure*, OECD Publishing, Paris, http://dx.doi.org/10.1787/9789264212664-en.

OECD (2015d), *Policy Framework for Investment 2015 Edition*, OECD Publishing, Paris. http://dx.doi.org/10.1787/9789264208667-en

OECD (2014a), *OECD Foreign Bribery Report - An Analysis of the Crime of Bribery of Foreign Public Officials*, OECD Publishing, Paris, http://dx.doi.org/10.1787/9789264226616-en.

OECD (2014b), "Toolkit on effective public investment across levels of government – Australia", www.oecd.org/effective-public-investment-toolkit/australia.pdf.

OECD (2014c), *Lobbyists, Governments and Public Trust, Volume 3: Implementing the OECD Principles for Transparency and Integrity in Lobbying*, OECD Publishing, Paris, http://dx.doi.org/10.1787/9789264214224-en.

OECD (2014d), "Recommendation of the Council on Effective Public Investment across Levels of Government", www.oecd.org/regional/regional-policy/Principles-Public-Investment.pdf.

OECD (2014e), *The Governance of Regulators*, OECD Publishing, Paris, http://dx.doi.org/10.1787/9789264209015-4-en.

OECD (2013a), *Public Procurement Review of the Mexican Institute of Social Security: Enhancing Efficiency and Integrity for Better Health Care*, OECD Public Governance Reviews, OECD Publishing, Paris, http://dx.doi.org/10.1787/9789264197480-en.

OECD (2013b), *Implementing the OECD Principles for Integrity in Public Procurement: Progress since 2008*, OECD Publishing, Paris, http://dx.doi.org/10.1787/9789264201385-en.

OECD (2013c), *Investing Together: Working Effectively across Levels of Government*, OECD Publishing, Paris, http://dx.doi.org/10.1787/9789264197022-en.

OECD (2012a), *OECD Integrity Review of Brazil: Managing Risks for a Cleaner Public Service*, OECD Public Governance Reviews, OECD Publishing, http://dx.doi.org/10.1787/9789264119321-en.

OECD (2012b), "Recommendation on Principles for Public Governance of Public-Private Partnerships", www.oecd.org/governance/budgeting/PPP-Recommendation.pdf.

OECD (2010), *Accountability and Transparency: A Guide for State Ownership, Corporate Governance*, OECD Publishing, Paris, http://dx.doi.org/10.1787/9789264056640-en.

OECD (2008), "Corruption: A Glossary of International Standards in Criminal Law".

OECD (2007a), *Integrity in Public Procurement: Good Practice from A to Z,* OECD Publishing, Paris, http://dx.doi.org/10.1787/9789264027510-en, pp. 79-80.

OECD (2007b), *Principles for Private Sector Participation in Infrastructure*", OECD Publishing, Paris, http://dx.doi.org/10.1787/9789264034105-en.

OECD (2006), *Policy Framework for Investment: A Review of Good Practices*, OECD Publishing, Paris, http://dx.doi.org/10.1787/9789264025875-en.

OECD (2004), "Framework for Investment Policy Transparency", in *International Investment Perspectives 2004*, OECD Publishing, Paris, http://dx.doi.org/10.1787/iip-2004-en

OECD (2003), "Checklist for Foreign Direct Investment Incentive Policies", www.oecd.org/investment/investment-policy/2506900.pdf.

OECD (1997), "OECD Convention on Combating Bribery of Foreign Public Officials in International Business Transactions", www.oecd.org/daf/anti-bribery/oecdantibriberyconvention.htm.

OECD, UNODC and World Bank (2013), *Anti-Corruption Ethics and Compliance Handbook for Business*, www.oecd.org/corruption/Anti-CorruptionEthicsComplianceHandbook.pdf.

PPPIRC (2014), *Main Financing Mechanisms for Infrastructure Projects*, http://ppp.worldbank.org/public-private-partnership/financing/mechanisms.

Public Works and Government Services Canada (2015), "Government of Canada's Integrity Regime", www.tpsgc-pwgsc.gc.ca/ci-if/ci-if-eng.html.

Public Works and Government Services Canada (2014), "Context and purpose of the Code", www.tpsgc-pwgsc.gc.ca/app-acq/cndt-cndct/contexte-context-eng.html.

Shoenherr (2013a), "Austria: Whistleblower hotline is launched online", www.schoenherr.eu/knowledge/knowledge-detail/austria-whistleblower-hotline-is-launched-online/.

Schoenherr (2013b), "Slovakia: Substantial changes in public procurement - Every detail counts", www.schoenherr.eu/knowledge/knowledge-detail/slovakia-substantial-changes-in-public-procurement-every-detail-counts/.

Thacher Associates (2013), "Tappan Zee Hudson River Crossing Project; Report of the Independent Procurement Integrity Monitor", www.newnybridge.com/documents/int-monitor-report.pdf.

Transparency International (2014), *Curbing Corruption in Public Procurement: A Practical Guide*, www.transparency.org/whatwedo/publication/curbing_corruption_in_public_procurement_a_practical_guide.

Transparency International (2013), "Whistleblowing in Europe", www.transparency.de/fileadmin/pdfs/Themen/Hinweisgebersysteme/EU_Whistleblower_Report_final_web.pdf, p. 25.

UNDP (n.d.), "UNDP/CIPS Cooperation on Procurement Training and Certification", www.undp.org/content/undp/en/home/operations/procurement/procurement_training.html (accessed on 20 October 2015).

UNESCO (2015), "The experience of the participative budget in Porto Alegre, Brazil", www.unesco.org/most/southa13.htm.

United States Government Accountability Office (2009), "Bid Protests at GAO: A Descriptive Guide", Ninth Edition, GAO-09-471SP, Washington DC, www.gao.gov/assets/210/203631.pdf.

Vodafone (n.d.), "Anti-bribery", http://vodafone360.com/content/index/about/about_us/suppliers/anti_bribery.html.

World Bank (2015), "Participatory budgeting in Brazil", *Empowerment Case Studies*, http://siteresources.worldbank.org/INTEMPOWERMENT/Resources/14657_Partic-Budg-Brazil-web.pdf.

WEF (World Economic Forum) (2015), *Mitigating Political and Regulatory Risk for Successful Infrastructure Projects*, www3.weforum.org/docs/Media/WEF_RM%20Report%202015.pdf.

ORGANISATION FOR ECONOMIC CO-OPERATION AND DEVELOPMENT

The OECD is a unique forum where governments work together to address the economic, social and environmental challenges of globalisation. The OECD is also at the forefront of efforts to understand and to help governments respond to new developments and concerns, such as corporate governance, the information economy and the challenges of an ageing population. The Organisation provides a setting where governments can compare policy experiences, seek answers to common problems, identify good practice and work to co-ordinate domestic and international policies.

The OECD member countries are: Australia, Austria, Belgium, Canada, Chile, the Czech Republic, Denmark, Estonia, Finland, France, Germany, Greece, Hungary, Iceland, Ireland, Israel, Italy, Japan, Korea, Luxembourg, Mexico, the Netherlands, New Zealand, Norway, Poland, Portugal, the Slovak Republic, Slovenia, Spain, Sweden, Switzerland, Turkey, the United Kingdom and the United States. The European Union takes part in the work of the OECD.

OECD Publishing disseminates widely the results of the Organisation's statistics gathering and research on economic, social and environmental issues, as well as the conventions, guidelines and standards agreed by its members.

OECD PUBLISHING, 2, rue André-Pascal, 75775 PARIS CEDEX 16
(42 2016 03 1 P) ISBN 978-92-64-25175-5 – 2016

www.ingramcontent.com/pod-product-compliance
Lightning Source LLC
LaVergne TN
LVHW081418110826
845149LV00010B/1789

* 9 7 8 9 2 6 4 2 5 1 7 5 5 *